RUBY TANDOH

EAT UP!

This paperback edition published in 2018

First published in Great Britain in 2018 by Serpent's Tail,
an imprint of Profile Books Ltd
3 Holford Yard
Bevin Way
London
WC1X 9HD
www.serpentstail.com

1 3 5 7 9 10 8 6 4 2

Typeset in Minion by MacGuru Ltd
Printed and bound in Great Britain by
CPI Group (UK) Ltd, Croydon CR0 4YY

A CIP catalogue record for this book is
available from the British Library.

ISBN 978 1 78125 960 3
eISBN 978 1 78283 407 6

Mixed Sources
Product group from well-managed
forests and other controlled sources
www.fsc.org Cert no. TT-COC-002227
© 1996 Forest Stewardship Council
FSC

Contents

'Everybody gotta eat, right?'

Common

Introduction

When our souls are happy, they talk about food.

Charles Simic

I often think about where food begins and ends. I don't necessarily mean the chronological beginning and end – the one-way march through time, from field to plate – although that certainly plays a part. I mean the whole picture. You're holding an iced ring doughnut in your hand – I mean the sticky edges where the doughnut meets skin, the long sweet history of beignets and crullers and cronuts, and the impulse to snack. I mean the science that turns heavy dough a deep orange hue when it hits the fryer, and the social currency of a doughnut box at work. Every mouthful of plain glazed Krispy Kreme ring or funfair cinnamon sugar doughnut is a bite of all of this – the human taste for sweetness, and a global doughnut love affair that's the making of us from the belly up.

Sometimes we lose all of this magic in the margins. Even though food is everywhere in our social fabric and in our culture, it's still squeezed into one thing or another. Diet gurus make food the sum of calories and carbs. Self-avowed foodies use food as a code for class. Restaurant critics polish food into a smooth, substance-less thing, while food writers like myself are guilty of constructing a fantasy food world that sits outside of real life. All of these conflicting ideologies mean that food is, in many ways, more complex and controversial than ever. We're sat right in the middle of a smorgasbord that stretches from Nevada to Nauru – trifles and meatballs and spare ribs teetering all around, wine flowing from fountains, all of the earth's bounty at the end of our forks – and we're too conflicted to take a bite.

Somehow, the most elemental, easy, joyful thing we can do has become a chore and a source of anxiety, and we begrudge these blurry boundaries that encroach on us when we take the outside world inside us, and make ourselves from the inside out. Food is the point where our bodies merge with the vast universe outside, and that's scary. So, as a society, we've created whole industries fighting that fear: 'natural foods', nutrient supplements, industrial farming, organic produce – all of these radically different, often contradictory, ideas are designed to give us a sense of control over this wild, delicate planet, and the bodies we inhabit. We don't want to go hungry, we don't want to be greedy, we don't want to live too exuberantly, we don't want to be a kill-joy. We fret about our size and shape, and too often police the bodies of others. We accept the lie that there's a perfect way of eating that will save your soul and send you careering blithely through your eighties, into your nineties and beyond. Do what you want, we're told – but you'll die if you get it wrong.

I don't want you to feel this way. Food shouldn't be a bad boyfriend, dragging you down or holding you to ransom. It should nourish your body as much as it fuels your mind; it should pump life through your veins; it should waltz in sync with your mood and your appetite, sometimes blissful, often mundane, always a part of you. This communion with food doesn't need to be something magical. In fact, part of making peace with your appetite is acknowledging that it's not always pretty, and sometimes you will enter a fugue state halfway through a packet of Cadbury Fingers and eat the lot and feel ill, and that's OK. Not every meal will be in some sunlight-dappled orange grove; sometimes what you need is a pasty by the side of the M4, and there's no harm in that.

I wrote this book as an antidote to all these confused, disjointed approaches to food. I don't want to tell you what to eat, how, when or where. There is no single 'right' way to eat, and you should be duly suspicious of anyone who tells you there is. What this book is about is everything that happens in the peripheries when we take a bite: the cultures that birth the foods we love, the people we nurture, the science of flavour and the ethics of eating. I've researched the tangled origins of some of our favourite foods, from waffles to Graham crackers, explored the place that we humans inhabit in the food chain, and looked at food anew through the lens of some of my favourite films. You can learn as much about food in five minutes of *Moonlight* as you can in five hours of *MasterChef*, and be nourished way more by Kelis's 'Milkshake' than a pint of Soylent.

I want you to eat the whole picture, because when you do that, food tastes better than ever. I want you to love yourself enough not to feed yourself dry sandwiches for dinner, or skip eating altogether. The way you feel about food sits hand in hand with the way you feel about yourself, and if you eat happily and wholeheartedly, food will make you strong. I want you to feel fine about the messiness of your illogical, impulsive appetite, and sometimes overeat, sometimes undereat, and still hold tight in your self-care. I want you to absorb as much of this big, weird world as possible. I want you to eat up.

The magic

Blackberrying

When I was eight or nine, my grandmother was living in a house in a sleepy Essex suburb. I often visited her with my younger siblings in tow, and we used to spend much of our stay in the garden. Granny's garden was her pride and joy, kept as neat as a guardsman's coat, the grass soft and verdant, shrubs blooming in bright colours. Granny kept order with a pair of garden shears, her eagle eyes, and a tub of slug pellets. When we went there during the summer, we were as carefully fussed over, preened and pruned as the roses and the rampant buddleia. I would stand in the sun, sipping orange juice and gripping the grass between my bare toes.

What I loved more than this garden, though, was the scrubby track that ran alongside it and out into the wood beyond. The track shrugged up against my grandmother's house and garden, its nettles, hollyhocks and tangles of thorns running shoulder to shoulder with the neatly coiffed gardenias and chrysanthemums, separated by the thinnest panels of a smart, stained wooden fence. When we walked along this track, I would linger over matted grey tufts of badger fur, an ant's nest, a pile of horse poo ... these things were a thousand times more interesting than Granny's perennials.

A few hundred yards along this mud trail were the blackberry bushes. They scrambled up the roadside, along fences and over ragged stone walls, thick with thorns and clusters of inky blackberries, some branches hanging low over the track, drooping heavily with fruit. One day, we traipsed along with old ice cream cartons and clustered around these brambles, pulling the fattest, darkest berries from the branch and throwing them, alternately, into our cartons and our mouths. Picking the perfect blackberry took some practice: the sweetest berries were the softest, and so the most likely to crush in your grip as you pinched them from the stem. You had to be careful, all the while whipping your hands back from the pricks of the thorns. Bright purple, sticky juice muddled with countless tiny cuts and grazes, which would sting hot all the way back home.

Once back from the abundant chaos of blackberrying, we washed our haul, tossed it with apple segments, sugar and cinnamon and covered it with a thick layer of sweet, nutty crumble. We baked the crumble during the heavy, languid hours of the afternoon. I can't remember what the crumble tasted like, in the end – whether the blackberries stained the topping with crimson juice, or whether the apples were blandly sweet, crisp or soggy. I have no idea whether we ate it with cream, or custard, or ice cream. What I can remember is the sting of those blackberry thorns, the herbal smell of dirt, juice and sap on my fingertips, and the precious warmth of a berry picked straight from a patch of midday sun.

I don't think it's any coincidence that one of my fondest food memories is one with roots spreading far beyond the kitchen table. There is so much more to eating than just eating. Eating is picking blackberries, or deciding to pick blackberries next week, or remembering blackberries you picked fifteen years ago. It is choosing a mango in the supermarket – one soft enough to hold a dimple when you press a thumb to its flesh – holding it to your nose, and taking a gulp of its heady scent. Eating is texting your housemate 'Let's get takeaway.' It's weighing up your options between the tarka dal and the Keralan fish stew, and taking the time to squint your eyes, smack your lips and taste-imagine your way to a decision. Eating is feeding someone else. Eating is toasting spices in a hot pan, folding whisked eggs into a cake batter, slowly cranking the handle of a tin opener around a can of tomato soup. Eating is standing in front of the empty fridge, willing inspiration to come. Eating is folding down every page corner in a new recipe book.

In order to eat well, we need to eat with every part of ourselves. We see, feel, sense, taste, touch, predict and imagine food long before it ever arrives on our fork. Every one of these experiences is a kind of emotional, sensorial aperitif. Food shows on TV are particularly good at this kind of drawn-out, teasing temptation: watch Nigella Lawson glide around her kitchen and you'll notice all the exaggerated sensations, from the loudness of cake batter plopping into a tin or an avocado raspingly scraped from its skin, to the shimmering light, rich colours and slow-motion tactility of it all. Ina Garten might take a journey to the deli to choose some lox herself, taking us with her to see the glistening fish and experience the bustle of New York City, then back to the serenity of her country kitchen. The choosing, the sorting, the serving: from this comes a story.

Giving food a story means giving a simple meal the power to become a lifelong memory, whether that story starts with dipping a net in a rock pool or heaving a trolley around Lidl on a Saturday morning. It's about engaging all of your senses, and letting food, body, craving and daydream all bleed into one. I often think about blackberrying and about my juice-stained fingers and that eventual apple and blackberry crumble, and what always hits me is the blurriness of it all: the act of eating stretched out from bramble to plate; juice dying my fingertips blood red; and the smell of cooking crumble, and how these smells – both thick and sweet – became one and the same in my memories of that day.

This is all well and good, of course, until it comes to weaving it into the fabric of ordinary, hectic everyday life. Take the time to cradle a jar of Dolmio and really *feel* it in Asda and you'll be there in aisle 5 all day. Engage all of your senses and smell, taste and touch your way along the pick and mix counter in Wilko and security will have you nicked. I got shouted out of a shop in Italy by a *nonno* once because I didn't realise that touching the fruit and veg wasn't the kind of tactile, immersive Italian gesture of food thoughtfulness that I thought it was. '*I ganti! I ganti!*' the grandad hollered after me, while a gaggle of suitably be-gloved women tutted at me from the zucchini.

But chances are that no matter how blasé you think you are about food, you're piecing together a web of food stories and sensations every time you go to eat. Raising a glass with your mates, closing out the ruckus of the pub around you and bringing the dishwasher-warm pint glass to your lips for the first sip of beer: this is a food ritual. It turns a lukewarm pint into some kind of rousing, fortifying nectar. Choosing the fullest-looking cheese and ham sandwich from Boots, or eating an Oreo biscuit just so – these are the things that make food so much more than just fuel. We use our imaginations to bring new life to the saddest slice of lunchmeat, reviving it with some sharp pickle and good bread. We play with our food. We use every one of our senses. When the moment comes to finally eat, we taste more clearly than ever.

Kitchen therapy

With all this in mind, it should come as little surprise that cooking plays a vital role in the way that we eat. It's an extension of eating, really, and every moment we spend in the kitchen chopping, peeling, stirring and slicing deepens our connection with the food we eventually put in our mouths.

And it's not just our relationship with food that benefits from this kind of mindful cooking and eating – we can also go some way to healing our relationships with ourselves, soothing our daily stresses and anxieties and bolstering our mental health in general.

Researchers at the University of Otago in New Zealand published a study in 2016 that showed that young people who took part in some kind of everyday creative activity – whether that was crochet or cooking new recipes – fell into an 'upward spiral', with their well-being, creativity and enthusiasm higher than those who hadn't done these kinds of activities. Anecdotally, that resonates: for me, just taking half an hour out of the day to be in the kitchen cooking, experimenting, tasting and feeling can be enough to drag me out of the slump of my depression. The difficult part is mustering the enthusiasm to drag myself into the kitchen in the first place.

And there might be something specific to cooking, above and beyond the healing properties of creative activity in general, that supports mental well-being. It's something that even the mental health care establishment is cottoning on to: cooking therapy, where people are guided through the processes of cooking a nourishing meal with the help of a trained therapist, is increasingly accepted as an alternative therapy. One suitably trendy class in east London promised 'Breaditation' a couple of years ago, which is easy to scoff at if you've never channelled the pure unyielding rage of a bad breakup into kneading your bread dough. The idea is that cooking – done properly – can improve self-esteem, teamwork skills and planning, all of which are crucial components of a robust 'toolbox' for coping with mental health problems.

A lot of these therapies have their roots in mindfulness – a concerted sensory awareness that reconnects you with your body, and your food – but the benefits go beyond just a fleeting moment of calm. Mindfulness when eating means employing all of your senses, and *feeling* as much as you *think*. Rather than using that overworked, exhausted cognitive part of your brain, and thinking hard about the craft of cooking, and the finer details of the things before you on the plate, you ought to be smelling, tasting, feeling, listening and seeing. A plate of cheese and crackers becomes a scattered Mondrian, the crunch of biscuit will echo in your skull and the sharp salt hit of cheese will creep across your tongue. Often, mindful eating is a tactic used to encourage people to eat less ('Listen to your stomach,' they say, 'and you'll realise you aren't even hungry'), but you can't really use it as a tool. Mindful eating is something that will sometimes awaken a fierce hunger inside of you, and other times have you satisfied after a single square of chocolate. It's a way of putting your mind back into your body and, just for a moment, letting yourself be.

Of course, cooking can be stressful. The last dregs of your will to live go down the drain with your curdled custard. Your ego falls as flat as the birthday cake you just spent three hours baking. Your kitchen is a rat-infested, windowless cupboard in a house running off electricity stolen from the streetlight outside. All of these have been my failure stories at various points during my life. And that's without even touching on the drudgery – the heavy, awful boredom – of cooking the same old midweek meal, or the gut-knotting tension of cooking to impress, or the sabotage of clamped-shut mouths and angry tears when it comes to feeding children. Cooking can be the worst.

It doesn't help that the narratives around cooking for pleasure – as opposed to cooking for sustenance or money – are all rooted in bougie rituals of going to the farmers' market, travelling the world for recipe ideas or spending an eternity making cute jars of damson jam. We live in a time when food is more polarised than ever, a huge chasm yawning between 'thoughtful', 'foodie' cooking on the one hand, and fast 'junk' food on the other. Those 'Breaditation' workshops – the preserve of wealthy cosmopolitan professionals – would be laughed out of the door by a baker who rises at 3am each day to earn a living. *Cooking* – that vital, everyday, normal thing – has been shoved to the sidelines by *cookery* – something ripe with connotations of craft and class. Because of this, we're inclined to think that making *salmorejo* is a more meditative act than piercing the film on a fish pie ready meal. Eating a lemon tart in Paris is imbued with more romance than an Eccles cake in a park café.

But the food narratives we create when we shop, cook and eat don't need to be exotic, expensive or rarefied. They shouldn't be estranged from the humdrum, ugly, familiar mess of everyday life. They don't even have to taste good. The important thing is giving yourself time to imagine your food, to touch, taste and smell the ingredients, and to really sink into the pleasure of eating. Take a few minutes to drown out the cognitive white noise of emails, to-do lists and stresses, and just cook. Focus on the coolness of a head of lettuce, and the sound of knife through crisp leaf as you cut a wedge. Shove your flatmate's dirty dishes to the corner of the kitchen so that you can sit and enjoy your spaghetti hoops in blissful, uncluttered calm. This kind of nourishment doesn't come with a price tag. Here are four kind-of recipes which will, I hope, make a fairy tale out of even the most humdrum meal.

Homemade tomato soup

You don't need to have personally grown and picked your own tomatoes, or bought them from some organic food store, for your tomato soup to soar. Gazpacho and *salmorejo* and Manhattan clam chowder all have their virtues, but you can find soup success far closer to home. The story starts in your local supermarket or corner shop, with a couple of tins of chopped tomatoes. Lay out your ingredients in front of you: the two tins of tomatoes, three cloves of garlic, the leaves from a bunch of fragrant basil, bottle of olive oil, some butter, caster sugar and salt. Turn on the radio, roll up your sleeves and turn off your phone: plant your mind and body firmly in the kitchen, and switch on all of your senses.

   Drizzle two or three tablespoons of the olive oil into a large saucepan. Dip your finger in it, and taste how light and peppery it is, then set it over a low heat. Watch how the oil – at first thick, glossy and smooth – begins to loosen, running across the base of the pan and shimmering more sharply as it gets hot. Add two tablespoons of butter, and watch it slide and bubble into molten gold. Peel the garlic cloves (let your fingers take on the smell of the garlic – it is a joy!) and crush them into the hot oil and butter. Stir immediately, keeping the garlic moving and taking in great lungfuls of that garlicky hit as it softens from sharp and astringent to mellow, sweet and rich. Listen as it sizzles. After a minute or so, add the basil leaves, pausing briefly to bruise one between your finger and thumb and hold it to your nose. Pour in the chopped tomatoes, add a teaspoon of sugar and 200ml of boiling water, put a lid on the pan, and simmer for 20 minutes, stirring occasionally. No need to blend this, but you're welcome to if you like a smoother soup. Season generously with salt – tomatoes really need this seasoning to come to life – and serve with crusty bread. Serves 2–3.

A Creme Egg ritual

Cadbury Creme Eggs aren't available all year round. They just appear sometime after the New Year, and are gone by the end of April and, as with all things with a short season – blushing pink forced rhubarb, blood oranges, tiny jewel-like blackcurrants – they're impossible to resist when they're around. It is a truth universally acknowledged that a Creme Egg in a special Easter display in mid-February just *has* to be bought and eaten, in case you never have the good fortune to happen upon another one.

Because they're a limited time offer, you have to make sure that you eat every Creme Egg as though it might be your last, even if you know perfectly well that you'll be rinsing the Londis across the road for them until every last egg is gone. To start, carefully choose your egg: rustle through the display until you find the only egg with a scannable barcode and its bright foil intact. Buy it, and slip it into your jacket pocket. Carry the egg with you all day, feeling the weight of it in your pocket, noticing it gently rolling around as you walk. Sit through meetings, lectures, coffee dates with your thoughts fixed on the heavy egg just within grabbing distance of your greedy fingertips. Imagine the waxiness of the chocolate on your lips. Think about dipping your tongue into the sickly sweet fondant inside and deftly, explicitly, licking it out.

Then, when the moment is right, eat.

Three-day whisky gingerbread loaf cake

Time is the secret ingredient here. I often make mug cakes that cook in the microwave, packets of cake mix that come with little rice paper cartoon characters to go on top, cheerful chocolate Rice Krispie cakes. All of these things are perfect in that moment, but sometimes I need a different kind of sweet fix. This cake will test your patience and your commitment to the cause: after baking, it needs a full three days of TLC before it's ready to eat. You'll need to swaddle it in foil, 'feed' it whisky and keep it safe from hungry hands as though nursing a small, boozy baby.

Preheat the oven to 180°C/fan 160°C/gas mark 4. In a medium saucepan set over a low heat, combine 75g each of salted butter and black treacle, and 100g of light brown sugar, and stir until melted and smooth. Take the pan off the heat, and whisk in 100ml of full-fat milk and two lightly beaten eggs. In a large bowl, mix 140g of plain flour, two teaspoons of ground ginger, half a teaspoon of ground cinnamon, half a teaspoon each of bicarbonate of soda and baking powder, and a good pinch of ground nutmeg. Pour the wet mixture slowly into the dry ingredients, stirring constantly until the batter is more or less smooth. Pour into a 2lb/900g loaf tin and bake for 30–40 minutes, or until a small knife inserted into the middle of the cake comes out clean. Immediately brush the top of the cake with a little whisky and leave to cool, then remove from the tin and wrap in kitchen foil.

Once a day, for two more days, unwrap the heavy little bundle and brush with a little bit more whisky. Smell the treacly, subtly boozy kick of the cake, and feel the springy, tender sides with your fingers. Imagine what it will taste like once it's had a chance to rest, and its flavour has matured. At the end of the third day, the cake is ready. Mix 125g of icing sugar with just enough whisky to make a smooth, pourable glaze, and stir in the zest of half an orange. Pour over the cake and leave to set for an hour or so. Once it's ready, slice the cake thickly, sit down and happily, hungrily *eat*. Big enough for 6–8 chunky slices.

I Hate My Husband Pie

> I Hate My Husband Pie: You take bittersweet chocolate
> and don't sweeten it. You make it into a pudding and
> drown it in caramel.
>
> *Waitress*

You might not have watched *Waitress*, but you should. In the
2007 indie rom-com, written and directed by the late Adrienne Shelly, small-town waitress Jenna deals with bad news
– her pregnancy by abusive husband, Earl, and an affair with
her doctor – by making good pie. Against the backdrop of the
drudgery and dead ends of her life, pie becomes an emblem
of something romantic, joyful and new. In baking scenes
dotted throughout the film, Jenna slides into wistful daydreams, imagining I Hate My Husband Pie, or Earl Murders
Me Because I'm Having An Affair Pie. Pie crusts made of
pastry, biscuits or chocolate crumb are heaped with custard,
mountains of meringue, marshmallow fluff, berries and dark
cocoa cream, to the tune of the film's tinkling, dream-like
soundtrack.

Baking has a particular power in our culinary landscape.
There's a reason why shows such as *The Great British Bake
Off* have been so incredibly popular, and why bake sales,
lazy Sunday bake sessions and café culture have run away
with our wallets. It was speculated in *Bake Off*'s heyday,
from around 2012 to 2016, that the boom in home baking
was thanks to a post-recession interest in low-cost hobbies.
Gone were the days of go-karting and theme parks: this was
a mini-era of pottering around with a rolling pin. But the
draw of cookies and cake and all this soft, domestic sweetness goes well beyond the push and pull of fiscal fortune.
From Isabella Beeton to Sylvester Graham (the puritanical
mind behind Graham crackers, more on him on pages 193–4),
Mary Berry to Nigella, baking is symbolic of a great deal

more than just golden crusts and soggy bottoms. When *How to Be a Domestic Goddess* was first released in 1998, it pretty much singlehandedly revived a cashmere-cloaked vision of homemaking femininity that many thought had been left for good in the 1950s. Mary Berry signalled a resurgence of interest in traditional British cooking at a time when the country as a whole, bolstered by right-wing nationalism, was growing unsure of exactly where to draw the line between 'us' and 'them'. But the most interesting kind of power that baking wields isn't big or political – it's in the aprons and oven gloves of the individual people who give it a go.

I like to see *Waitress* as a kind of case study of this power. When Jenna slips into baking she steps out of the turmoil of her situation and into a place where everything is as sweet, safe and homely as pie. This is pure nostalgia: diner culture, waitresses in sky blue frocks and aprons, small-town life. Pie is itself a United States institution, as all-American as stars and stripes. With every pie she bakes, Jenna claws back a scrap of so-called normality, and allows herself, in defiance of her abusive husband, to be nostalgic, generous and soft. The alleged 'girliness' of baking – that it asks us to be careful, make things pretty, practise precision and celebrate sweetness – is sometimes used as a stick to beat home bakers with, but it's actually baking's biggest draw. In what other part of our cluttered lives do we have a moment to just bask in beauty and sweetness and delicacy? Baking is an escape.

Of course, there is no physiological *need* for baking, but that's precisely its appeal: in a world where so much of what we do is in the name of achieving some end, baking is just pleasure in and of itself. It's special because we don't need it, but we want it, and we allow ourselves to indulge that appetite nonetheless. With deadlines creeping and bills climbing and relationships shuddering to a halt, we can take a step aside from all of that humdrum mess and make something sweet. The fact that baking takes so long only makes it more special, because it cannot be rushed. It can't be squeezed into the half-hour between work and gym. 'I have my four-hour morning ahead, whole as a pie,' Sylvia Plath once wrote, having left her prestigious teaching job, and finding herself free to write, bake and slowly coax herself back into a softer kind of life.

Just how to start baking is a tricky question. It's a scary thing: much less intuitive than other kinds of cooking, and far easier to mess up. Plenty of people swear off ever even trying, or tie their whole worth to one lacklustre apple crumble they made in food tech in year eight. But it really doesn't have to be a big deal. The whole point of it is that nothing hinges on your baking success or failure. You won't go hungry if it all goes wrong, because cake was never going to form the back-bone of your diet in the first place. And whatever happens, you'll still get to lick the bowl. This is food for food's sake – for tasting, chewing, smelling, savouring and delighting in every last atom of goodness. But, if you're going to start anywhere, pie is as good a place as any. Unlike cakes (where success depends on care and balance) or biscuits (which so easily turn from doughy lumps to brittle rusks with just a few too many minutes in the oven), pies are there for the taking in the hands of even the most hapless baking novice. Even the chewiest pie crust is heaven when its underneath is sodden with a shock of blackberry juice. A not-quite-set apple custard filling is still sweet, nutmeg-laced joy.

Stone a bowlful of cherries, whisk some cream into snowy white peaks, crumble butter and flour with your hands. Make the most beautiful pie, and fill it with love, or bitterness, or jealousy, or whatever thoughts and feelings are flooding your mind. It doesn't really matter if it works or what goes in it. Stuff an Oreo crust with chocolate cream filling. Lay a pastry lid over an apple pie so full that the crust bulges like a pregnant belly. Bake your pie perfectly with a glazed lattice crust, or burn it out of spite. You don't even have to eat a mouthful of it. Make a key lime pie, top it with great swirls of meringue, then pie the face of someone you really hate (it doesn't have to be your husband).

Boiled eggs

I spend so much time cooking, but I don't really know what happens inside a frying pan or in the oven. I make my sauce or meringue or cake or stew and I just trust that my care will somehow take the food from raw ingredients to finished meal. Much of what actually happens on a smaller scale – in among the molecules, granules and squishy bits – is a mystery to me. And so much *does* happen when we cook. You don't even have to look to high cuisine or molecular gastronomy to find magic in cooking. Every piece of supermarket Cheddar contains countless configurations of chemical elements and compounds, all woven together in an impossibly tiny universe of *stuff* that forms the proteins, fats, minerals and salts that, in turn, make up the cheese itself.

There's one dish that I make weekly, sometimes more: a tomato sauce for pasta, from a recipe by Italian-born food writer Marcella Hazan. So many people will tell you that a good pasta sauce needs richness from olive oil, garlic and herbs. They insist that in order for a meal to taste good, it needs to be made of the best stuff, the 'best' unfailingly being – no surprises here – the most expensive. That means trudging to the market for heavy, bursting, scarlet red tomatoes: the kind that come still on the vine, the herbal, nostalgic smell of sun on their skins. Hazan has an alternative. In her recipe, you simply combine two tins of chopped tomatoes, an onion – peeled and halved – and a sizeable chunk of butter. Cook over a medium–low heat for 45 minutes, then remove the onion, season with salt, and serve. I don't know how, from such store-cupboard basics, comes such a luxuriantly thick, rich, buttery, savoury sauce. The sharpness of those watery tinned tomatoes softens into sweet, crimson velvet, making a sauce that's infinitely more than the sum of its parts. All it takes is a long, slow cook.

This kind of transformation is exactly what makes cooking so enduringly fascinating, no matter how many meals you've made. Take, for example, a bread roll – even a cheap, squashed, bottom-of-the-rucksack bread roll. This bread roll is a miracle. The bare elements of bread are just flour, water, yeast and salt, but the stuff that turns those raw ingredients into a light, sweet, perfect bap are as complicated as moon missions, evolutionary biology and taxes. Yeast is a fungus that, when rehydrated and given carbohydrates to 'eat', releases millions of tiny bubbles of carbon dioxide and a dash of alcohol. This turns a lifeless lump of dough into a sort of living, breathing thing, that grows and grows and grows until the yeast has nothing left to give.

And the magic doesn't stop there. When the bread hits the oven, proteins and sugars in the dough transform in what is maybe my favourite chemical reaction of all time: the Maillard reaction. It gives that lovely, slightly chewy, golden top to a loaf of bread, as well as all these things: the rich, sweet, browned layer on the very outside of a steak cooked to perfection; the soft upper edge of a Madeira cake, that melts on your tongue; onions collapsing into a caramelised, sticky tangle in a butter-slicked pan; *dulce de leche*, scooped by a finger straight from the jar; the chewy, salty, mahogany crust of a fresh-baked pretzel. This complex, wondrous chemistry even makes an appearance at the breakfast table. While your eyes are still heavy with sleep, it's there in your mug of coffee, your breakfast cereals, and even in the pleasure of a slice of perfectly golden-brown, buttered toast. It doesn't matter how culinarily skilled (or otherwise) you are – if you can make toast, you're a modern-day alchemist.

There are plenty of other varieties of kitchen chemistry, of course. When you fry minced beef, it's the oxidisation of the iron in the mineral-rich meat that turns it from blood-red to brown. Or think of a banana ripening, turning from a starchy, potato-like substance, firm and unyielding in its tight green skin, to something tender, blackened and as sweet as toffee. As it ripens, the banana releases a chemical called ethylene, which helps other fruit around it to ripen. There's even something special about the moment when, as you push a handful of spaghetti into a pan of boiling water, the spaghetti strands rehydrate, yield and collapse and curl slowly down into the pot. I'm forever cursed by that split second in the microwave when a mug of milk goes from lukewarm to stickily, impossibly, infuriatingly boiled over. That happens because water evaporating at the milk's surface leaves behind a thicker, more concentrated layer of milk fat and solids, under which air bubbles get trapped when the milk boils.

All of these things are amazing. Most amazing of all, however, is a very simple food. The whole joy of cooking is contained within it, and the boundless possibilities of food open up in front of us when we crack it open. I'm talking about eggs.

Until last year, I had never boiled an egg. Even now, I can retain in the murky corners of my mind the full recipes for lemon meringue roulade, butter maple ice cream, Catalan fish stew spiked with garlic and saffron, but I can't for the life of me remember exactly how to cook an egg. I am always typing 'Delia soft-boiled egg' into Google, cutting straight to the authoritative voice of simple cookery. Are you meant to put the eggs into boiling water or cold? Do you boil them or simmer them or turn the heat down so low that they barely stir? I know that you absolutely should – or absolutely should not – put the eggs in the pan straight from the fridge, but I just cannot, will not, remember which it is.

(As it happens, I have just Googled how to cook a soft-boiled egg for the millionth time and the trick is to put room-temperature eggs in cool water, bring to the boil and simmer for 1 minute. Turn off the heat, put a lid on the pan and leave to sit for precisely 6 minutes for a perfectly runny yolk.)

Somehow out of the gummy white and the rich yolk come buttery sandwich cakes, the mahogany sheen of an egg-glazed brioche, omelettes laden with French cheese and tufts of fresh spring herbs, clouds of sweet meringue, towering (and tumbling) soufflés and silky vanilla-speckled custard, not to mention marshmallows browning over an open flame, pots of sweet-spicy *shakshuka*, and honey madeleines. An egg can bind, puff, gel, lighten, set, enrich and garnish everything from chocolate éclairs to heavy pots of velvety crème brulée. Despite egg whites being almost entirely made of water, the 10% protein they contain makes them capable of whipping into a dense foam: the foundation of everything from sponge cake to meringue. The fattiness of yolks makes them rich and delicious, while a protein in them called lecithin is the stuff that helps to bind oil and water together in mayonnaise, forming an emulsion. I was vegan for just under a year when I first started university, and it was eggs I missed the most: they're in *everything*, and they're magic.

What's more, there's no knowing an egg until you've broken it. There could be two deep orange yolks or a single one as fat and yellow as a buttercup. When it's boiled, there's no way to tell if the egg is runny or set, with a yolk that's smooth, thick and liquid, fudgy, or the texture of a rubber boot. Food writer M. F. K. Fisher famously wrote: 'Probably one of the most private things in the world is an egg before it is broken.' That's just the trouble with eggs. As with so many good things, you never really know what blessings you've got until something, or someone, gets broken.

No wonder that egg is at the heart of some of our most healing meals. A boiled egg with soldiers is a panacea for the weak and weary, while scrambled eggs can soften even the bleakest hangover. Egg fried rice is an elixir for my girlfriend when her mental or physical health is waning. Some people even drink raw eggs, Rocky Balboa-style, as workout fuel. (Those people are sociopaths, I'm sorry to say.) Every domestic goddess from Isabella Beeton to Julia Child and Delia Smith has schooled us in the ways of cooking omelettes, poached eggs, eggs en cocotte and boiled eggs. The British Egg Information Service – surely the source of all glitz and glamour in the egg world – even ran the famous 'Go to work on an egg' campaign from 1957 to 1971 in a bid to show that eggs were everything a salt-of-the-earth, good-and-honest person could need in the morning.

Follow an egg down the road less travelled – not to the plate, but to the chicken coop, nestled safe under the bum of a doting mother hen – and a whole new story unfolds. When fertilised and incubated, a single, simple egg creates a whole new life. It is the sign of Easter rebirth, fertility, resurrection, abundance and even life itself, depending on where in the world you're from. Some historic forms of fortune-telling have involved 'reading' the form of a cracked egg white. Certain Hindu cosmologies have it that the whole universe had its origins in a golden egg. If someone has cooked eggs for you, they have loved you, and it is impossible not to fall in love with them in return. The egg is all of life condensed into one smooth, ovoid shell: it is the alpha and the omegga.

It makes sense then, given all the wonder that the humble egg contains, that it should also be a building block for things far bigger than just omelettes. The egg is where I turn when the kitchen has become a stale, stifling place, when I'm deep in the food rut and no longer see magic in the meals I cook. Eggs are a reminder of all the weird, magical chemistry contained within every bite we eat. Next time you're flummoxed for meal ideas in the kitchen, think eggs. Hold an egg in the palm of your hand and remember that it is a capsule of pure potential: if you have eggs in the house, you have dinner, no matter how bare your kitchen cupboards. Often, when I'm raiding the fridge for a weekday dinner, I heat up whatever leftovers I have – whether it's jollof rice or stewed aubergine with spices and spinach – and just serve with a fried egg on top. Somehow, a single egg makes the whole dish sing anew.

Hungry human bodies

Food in the frame

Food is everywhere in art. There's a painting in Tate Britain, for instance, called *Cookmaid with Still Life of Vegetables and Fruit*, painted around 1620 by Sir Nathaniel Bacon. In this luxuriantly colourful, detailed work – so large that when you stand in front of it, you can scarcely take it all in at once – a buxom cook reclines winsomely against a wall, surrounded by an abundance of fruit, vegetables and flowers. To her left there's a basket piled high with figs, peaches, apples and plums; from the right-hand side of the painting sprout four or five of the biggest cabbages I've ever seen, each of their unfurling, wrinkled leaves as big as a small child. I'm not joking when I say that the maid holds a massive melon to her ample chest. It's hardly subtle, but that's what this kind of symbolic excess is all about: a celebration of wealth, plenty, and full-chested womanliness, regardless of the reality of what it means to harvest, cook and eat the haul at hand.

But do you know how hard it is to find artworks that show people eating? It's an impossible task. Food is everywhere, in the old masters and even in the strange, difficult, modern art of the here and now, but good luck finding a painting of someone actually taking a bite of something. Even in Da Vinci's *The Last Supper*, none of the thirteen figures at the table are taking the opportunity to actually eat. People make a living from taking photos of the food they eat in the restaurants they visit, and posting these snaps online, and yet we seldom see these self-declared gourmands take a single bite. Eating doesn't seem to have the same magnetism as the symbolic potency of the foods themselves. The eating of a burger is pretty quotidian, and not really the preserve of art, presumably. And yet a burger that acts as a metaphor for the greed of the Western world – somehow that's easier to stomach. I can't help wondering whether our own pride is tied up in this strange double-edged view of food. Eating is a messy act. Anyone who's ever been tagged in a photo on Facebook after a meal out will know the thumping panic of seeing themselves mid-mouthful, spinach in the cracks of their teeth, jaw twisted. There's no dignity in salivating, biting, chewing, swallowing, digesting, gurgling, burping and shitting. As much as we'd like to preserve some image of ourselves as pristine visions of faultless human glory, we're actually pretty gross. To eat is to admit that we are part of all the mess and madness of the world, and maybe that's something we don't want documented for posterity.

But the truth of the matter is that, much as we might like to think of ourselves as spiritual, emotional beings, on some level at least we are cells, atoms, dirt, germs, matter. We are made of *stuff*. Something as resolutely physical as food – pure, heavy stuff, from dirt-caked potatoes to the chips on your plate – can't feed, fuel or cure us or give us pleasure unless we, too, exist in that material world. While you read that poetry book or catch up on *The Fall* or engage in some blindingly clever philosophical musings, your body stays rooted in your chair, on this earth, doing all the wonderful, complex, disgusting, smelly things that bodies do. At some point in your intellectual pursuits, sooner or later, you'll be brought back into your body by a rude gurgle from your belly or a craving for something sweet. Your body is hungry for more. We're all messy, hungry human bodies, in the end.

Digest this

So, food anchors us in this world. It's something that earths us, even when our heads are in the clouds. We are animals, which means that we need energy from food in order to stay alive. It's a crucial daily reminder that we are finite, physical things. The ways in which our bodies mould to our food, and our food to our bodies, are, I think, some of the most incredible transformations that nature can offer up. Forget shooting stars or snakes slipping out of their skins, the way that something as unremarkable as a floppy petrol-station cheese sandwich can go from its packet, to a salty sharpness on your tongue, to the very fabric of your moving, breathing, living human body: that's magic. Just how does this sorcery unfold, though?

In a way, it would make sense to start this story with the mouth. The mouth is, after all, the official starting point of your food's journey through your digestive system, before it gulps into your oesophagus and tumbles into your stomach and through the metres of your intestine. We begin to mix our bodies with our food the second that it touches our lips, with enzymes in our saliva breaking down the starches in our food long before it ever reaches our stomachs. But I want to look at hunger first. Because somehow, the feeling of your belly rumbling, or the prickling excitement that floods your mouth at the thought of a great meal – these things are, to me, the purest reminders of what it means to eat.

Hunger is a sensation that we all experience at some point. It's the feeling that you need to eat, although beyond this it's difficult to find much consensus about exactly what 'real' hunger is. Common opinion has it that hunger is the physiological need to eat, whereas appetite is framed as just a desire to eat, driven by emotional or sensory pleasure rather than bodily need. We see this in the division between nutrition and gastronomy, or between food as fuel and food as pleasure. If it is really the case, then it should be easy to differentiate between 'real' hunger and its imposter, the greedy pangs of appetite. After that greasy burger and those salty, paprika-dusted curly fries, you should be able to recline, accept your satiety and graciously decline the dessert menu. But all too often, that's not how things work.

Certainly, there are times when you feel so full that it's as if the food is piled all the way up to your throat, and you can recognise that niggling desire for an After Eight as the super-fluous pleasure-seeking that it is. And, of course, you know in your heart that a bowl of porridge will better sate your morning hunger than the Mars Bar your appetite is veering towards. But just as often as they diverge, this physical hunger and psychological, sensory appetite merge into one. In reality, we find it hard to pick apart the particular craving we have for cheese on toast from the bodily needs that drive it. We might start a bowl of pasta to satisfy a hunger, and finish it to satisfy our senses. If it were that easy to pull pure hunger apart from extraneous craving, life would be very functional, and very dull.

Consider what's frequently brushed off as greedy, hedonis-tic appetite, for instance – namely, the desire to eat things that taste good and make us happy, such as a pint of cold beer and a plate laden with curry, or a bowl of ice cream squeezed in after a full roast dinner. For some, that's completely different from the hunger that rattles our stomachs in uncomfortable pangs when we've been working so hard we've skipped lunch. And yet, experience attests to the fact that our primary cri-terion in choosing food is not how it will satisfy our hunger at all, but how it tastes. Here in the UK, where food is plenti-ful, and so many of us are guided by questions of pleasure in our day-to-day decisions about food, it's just not possible to draw a clear line between 'fun' pleasure-eating and some kind of mythic 'true' hunger. Those distinctions just don't make sense.

The pleasure principle

So, pleasure is key to our decisions about what we eat and when. We're rarely just hungry for any old carbohydrate, for instance. Instead, we'll be hungry for buttery mashed potato, a heavy bowl of saffron risotto or a toasted hot cross bun. And sensory, pleasure-centric appetite doesn't just serve to make our gustatory lives more enjoyable, it can actually improve the nutritional quality of our diets.

A famous study conducted in the mid-1970s can shine a light on this. In the study, two groups of women – one Thai, the other Swedish – were fed a rice dish made using flavours and ingredients popular in Thai cooking. Researchers then monitored how much iron each of the groups of women was able to absorb from the meal, supposing that this mineral uptake would indicate how well the women were able to digest, and be nourished by, the food. The results were startling. The Thai women, who were more at ease with the spiciness of the food than the Swedish group, absorbed nearly 50% more iron than the Swedes. What's more, when, in another study conducted by the scientists, participants were fed the foods they knew and liked, first in the format they enjoyed, and then in a less appetising, but nutritionally identical, puréed format, the researchers discovered an even greater disparity in nutritional absorption. The women absorbed on average 70% less iron when they consumed the puréed foods than when they were able to appreciate the tastes, textures and sight of the meals in their usual presentation.

What these studies suggest is that the enjoyment we get from our food is intimately connected to the nutritional power of that food. Pleasure isn't just a happy side effect of following your appetite, then – it can be something that keeps us healthy. In a study conducted by Fifth Sense, a charity for those who suffer from a loss of smell or taste, it was found that 43% of people suffering from anosmia – a loss

of smell, which almost obliterates the capacity to taste different flavours – experienced depression, and 92% a decreased
appreciation of food and drink. Anosmia also carries with
it a risk of malnutrition, weight loss or gain, as those who
live with it struggle to maintain an interest in eating, once
so much of the pleasure has been stripped from it. There is
even the risk of food poisoning, as people with anosmia can't
discern rancid or 'off' foods from those that will do them
good. Clearly our ability to smell and taste isn't just an aesthetic benefit, but a physiological necessity: with a nose for
good food, the fulfilment of a basic human need – namely,
the need to feed – becomes something that we can pursue
fully, enthusiastically, and with pleasure.

And even when the food itself is to our taste, the context
of our eating has a huge bearing on our bodies' ability to
properly process and digest that food. Stress can suppress
our appetites, dry our mouths, cause indigestion, and lead to
diarrhoea or constipation. Imagine sitting down to breakfast
before a big exam. In front of you is a plate of thickly sliced
bread, toasted to a mottled gold and heavy with melting salted
butter. Maybe you've spread sweet strawberry jam on the
toast, too, or Marmite, or fragrant blossom honey. Anxious
about the looming exam, you hurriedly guzzle the toast,
but you barely taste it, and you certainly don't enjoy it. This
inoffensive piece of toast will come back to haunt you, about
fifteen minutes before your exam, when your belly swells to
a pregnant bloat. Maybe you'll need to rush to the bathroom,
or maybe you'll spend the exam trying to concentrate while
smuggling silent farts. Who can tell? The point is that when
you eat during stress and upset, that psychological anxiety
can manifest itself as physical malaise.

The link goes the other way too: in recent years, more and
more conversations have been had about the role of the gut
in brain health, to the degree that the gut has been dubbed

the 'second brain' by some nutritionists. There's some evidence to suggest that imbalances in the microbes in the gut can set off a chain reaction that may also lead to problems with things like concentration and cognitive ability, and even brain development. This science is comparatively new, though, and especially in light of some of the more unscrupulous 'nutritionists' out there (one so-called scientist called Natasha Campbell-McBride came to notoriety after claiming that Alzheimer's, autism and more could be managed, even cured, by a grain-free diet), it's worth exercising caution before completely overhauling your diet. Whatever comes of these new scientific insights, it's clear that the brain and the gut are rather unromantically allied, and what goes wrong with your thoughts can easily turn the fortunes of your belly, too.

It's not just what you eat, then, it's how you eat it. Eating food that you enjoy, in a context that's relaxed and pleasurable, is a step towards more efficient digestion and better health. Of course, not every sausage roll that you hanker after will be in your body's best interests, nor will every vitamin-packed smoothie necessarily get your tastebuds leaping for joy. But there's a lot of comfort in knowing that your appetite and your health needn't act at odds with one another. Sometimes, you can just sit back and trust your appetite to lead the way. Dietitian Ellyn Satter has a quote on the front page of her website: 'When the joy goes out of eating, nutrition suffers.' It's a thought that captures what should be a self-evident truth of eating: that it does us good to feel good. I'll talk more about Ellyn Satter and the principles of intuitive eating that she proposes elsewhere in this book, but for now just let her little catchphrase take root in your mind. Take it to the table with you this evening and let it fill your plate with things that awaken your senses. Follow your greedy, fickle, frivolous appetite where it leads.

Feel-good food

My girlfriend had a horrible cold recently. When Leah's sickness was just beginning to take root, burrowing into her sinuses and throbbing in her head, I made her a smoothie. I made it with fresh ginger, orange juice, big chunks of frozen mango, carrots and green apple, and poured it into her Thermos flask so she could sip it at work. I cooked her a warming soup that day, too, packed with all the veg that her ailing body probably needed. I gave her mugs of acrid-smelling, syrupy cold and flu remedy, and steady doses of herbal tea, and prescribed an early bedtime. I was sure she'd wake up the next day feeling better for all the love and vitamins I had sent her way, and as she sank into sleep with a wad of tissue bunged up one nostril, I graciously laid a healing hand over her heavy head and congratulated myself on a job well done.

The next morning, both Leah and I woke up foggy-headed and shivering. Cocooned in blankets and surrounded by a constellation of scrunched-up tissues, we lay in the living room all day watching old episodes of *Come Dine with Me*, drinking hot water and lemon, and praying for death. We did everything our mums would've asked us to – hot showers, hydration, soup, hydration, rest, hydration – and grew weaker by the hour. By mid-afternoon, Leah was so frail that she gagged when she tried to swallow a paracetamol, and it looked like we'd just have to let this sickness run its course.

But sometimes, at the gates of death, you get a flash of divine light and see all the beauty of the world and all the hope that's left to live for. In that moment, teetering at the pearly gates, so close that you can almost feel the candy floss clouds beneath your feet, you see your glorious future unfurl around you, and you decide to stomp right back into life and seize the day. That's exactly what happened when, ten minutes after gagging on a pill and turning down a cup of tea,

Leah turned to me with an unfathomable light behind her eyes and said: 'I have ordered £30 of Indian food on Just Eat.'

With numbed tastebuds and blocked noses, we ate like queens. We had Bombay fish curry (a fiery hot, creamy sauce, rich with chunks of tender mackerel), which came, as everything does on that takeaway menu, 'especially recommended by Abdul'. We wolfed fluffy, steaming rice with heaps of garlicky tarka dal, and between spoonfuls nibbled on spicy chicken wings, bright with lime and coriander and the punch of fresh red chilli. We ate with ferocious delight until we could eat no more. Our heads were still pounding, our bodies still bristled with goosebumps, and our skin was still tender to the touch. But for an hour or two, reclining in a happy, burping, bloated haze, we felt alive again.

It doesn't have to be a blow-out curry, of course: you can feel better again with a slice of dry toast or a teetering mountain of soft-baked fudge brownies, depending on your mood. It might be that a bowl of chicken soup or shepherd's pie is what you need to revive your spirits, or it could be – flying in the face of every piece of mum-wisdom you've ever been given – that what you really need is one of those McDonald's milkshakes that drags through the straw and coats your mouth and catches in your throat with delicious, saccharine glee. (For what it's worth, it's been shown that dairy doesn't actually increase mucus production after all, and any association between consumption of dairy and coughs has been shown to be negligible.) These foods might not be packed with precisely the vitamins and minerals and macronutrients that your body really needs right then and there, but they will make your soul soar, and sometimes – when the very fabric of your life is one big snotty tissue – that's all you really need.

Marvellous medicine

'But what about my gout?' I hear you cry. 'What about diabetes and high blood pressure and anaemia? Are you saying you can worm your way out of scurvy with a fish curry and some positive thinking?' Well, no. There are times when just *feeling* better is enough to *get* better – this is how Abdul's fish curry can help you through a cold, or a mug of thick hot chocolate before bed can drown out those insomniac anxieties for a night. In some cases, the psychosomatic element of some illnesses and ailments can be just as potent as the physiological cause. A 2003 study found that people with more positive emotional approaches to life were less susceptible to common cold viruses, while those who were more prone to negative emotions reported more symptoms, including unfounded symptoms, when exposed to the viruses. With that in mind, it's not impossible that eating something that makes you happy, which floods your wearied senses with pleasure or, at the very least, distracts you from your sickness, can be enough to put you on the road to recovery.

But not all sickness is this suggestible, and sometimes the body needs specific nutritional tools to help fuel its fight against microbes, immune disorders and so many of the other myriad strains that we endure each day just by virtue of existing, and surviving, in a stressful world. We take in nutrients from our food, and those nutrients – from the building blocks of carbohydrate, protein and fat, to minute doses of vitamins and minerals – are used by our bodies to keep us healthy, strong and well. Eat citrus fruits to keep your vitamin C levels up, and boost your immune system; boost your iron intake with leafy greens if you don't eat red meat, or you might risk anaemia. This is cause and effect at its most fundamental: goodness on your plate will help to foster goodness in your body. It's the idea that food can be medicine, rather than just fuel, and that, with a bit of fine-tuning and the right cocktail of nutrients, we can not only keep ourselves alive and well, but actually optimise the ways that our bodies function.

This quest for health doesn't need to be some joyless equation, though. Food is both fuel and medicine, but this doesn't mean we have to strip it bare of its magic and reframe it as a power source for some robot-like, maximally efficient human body. Yes, the reality is that food is a basic, physical human need. It is fuel, in a sense, and by extension, we are machines that need fuelling. But we're also thoughtful aesthetes who enjoy things like the smell of the sea air, and *Buffy* reruns, and pub quizzes. Our bodies are not just heavy machines that we drag around with us, and our gastronomic pleasure isn't just an aside when it comes to the mechanics of eating. Food can be medicine, and still be a joy. With that in mind, and because I want you to have the bliss of tasting delicious things, no matter the state of your health, here are a few meal ideas – with some notes on their medicinal properties – to help you feel good about staying well. Take the medicines your doctor gives you, don't forget to get your five a day and do your exercise. But have a little fun with your mealtimes, too.

Chicken soup for the common cold

When I first thought about food and bodies, I couldn't get the idea of healing chicken soup out of my mind. I wanted to write an ode to Jewish mums' chicken soups – their prized penicillin – and my girlfriend's Filipina mum's chicken *tinola*. The medicinal power of chicken soup is real. Studies show that carnosine, a compound found in chicken, reduces inflammation of the respiratory tracts, alleviating those 'blocked up' feelings in your head. The steam and heat of the soup, meanwhile, can clear the nose, and vitamins and minerals in the chicken bones and in the broth's vegetables can help to boost antibody production. But what's really magical about chicken soup isn't the nutrient quota or the fact it shifts your snot along: it's that it is a delicious, precious metaphor for caring, and for nourishing. What feels really good about feeding yourself chicken soup – whether it's a bone broth simmered for 12 hours or a microwaved bowl of Campbell's Cream of Chicken – is that it represents one small, crucial act of self-care.

Here's a chicken soup you can make yourself at home, if you're feeling under the weather and you've got some time to kill. It starts with the simple joy of sticking a whole chicken in a stockpot with water, salt and pepper, chopped carrots, two onions (peeled and halved), bay leaves, chunks of celery and a bunch each of parsley and dill. There's something magical about how this motley assortment of bits in a pan becomes, after some 2–3 hours of gentle simmering, a smooth, flavourful chicken soup. Skim off any scum or froth that collects on top as it cooks. Relish the brutal pleasure of shredding the flesh from the bone, filling a bowl and letting that meaty elixir soothe your soul.

Hazelnut porridge for diabetes

For those living with diabetes, it's important to keep blood sugar levels as stable as possible. That means avoiding foods that are high in simple sugars, such as sweets, chocolates and fizzy drinks, and trying to balance sugar intake with slower-release carbohydrates, proteins and fats. That's not always easy, especially at breakfast time when hunger strikes with that particular urgency, and so many of the usual foods on offer are sweet treats: Belgian waffles heaped with whipped mascarpone and summer berries, blueberry pancakes drizzled with maple syrup, granola clusters so sugar-packed that they leave me woozy.

There is another way, though. Ground roasted hazelnuts bring a mellow, nutty sweetness to porridge without the need to add any extra sugar at all, making a frugal breakfast into a feast.

Preheat the oven to 180°C/fan 160°C/gas mark 4. Roast a small packet of blanched hazelnuts in the oven for 10 minutes or so, until they're golden and fragrant, then grind to a fine powder in a food processor or coffee grinder (some supermarkets sell them ready roasted and ground). Combine the hazelnuts with 200g of porridge oats, a pinch of salt, 850ml of milk and 1½ mugs of water in a large, heavy-based pan and set over a medium heat. Stir the porridge often, and once it reaches a simmer, cook for a couple of minutes before serving with berries and, if you like, a drizzle of cream. Serves four.

A potato feast for coeliac disease

Gluten-free living is in vogue at the moment, and because that movement has very little to do with coeliac disease, and a lot to do with rebranding fad diets, it's easy to come away with the sense that a gluten-free diet is a lean, glossy-haired, dazzlingly low-calorie one. Well, it doesn't have to be. Coeliac disease, and the slightly more common non-coeliac gluten sensitivity, or NCGS, are both conditions that affect the body's ability to process the protein gluten, which is found in, among other things, wheat, barley and rye. If you suffer from coeliac disease or NCGS, avoiding foods that contain gluten is vitally important, because they can wreak havoc on your digestive health. That makes a lot of things off limits, including traditional forms of pasta and bread, cakes and flour-thickened sauces. And yet it doesn't have to mean a descent into some terrifying, sanitised, 'clean' eating, no matter what the self-styled nutritionist entrepreneurs would have you believe. You can eat heavy, messy, sticky, salty, sweet, cheesy, cloying, fatty, irresistible food. You can eat chips and potatoes and ice cream and meat. You can sit in front of the campfire with toasted marshmallow melted into your beard because, goddammit, life goes on. The world is still rich and delicious and full of flavour.

A coeliac-friendly meal I urge you to cook is potato dauphinoise. Make as much or as little as you need to feed yourself and your family or friends. Preheat the oven to 220°C/fan 200°C/gas mark 7. Cut your potatoes – you could mix the usual Maris Pipers with

sweet potatoes for colour and flavour – into slices as thick as a
£1 coin. Bring them to a simmer in a saucepan of milk seasoned
with a peeled clove of garlic, a scraping of nutmeg, some salt and
pepper, and a bay leaf or two. Arrange the potato slices in layers in
a baking dish, scattering fistfuls of Gruyère or Cheddar cheese over
each layer, and drizzling the milk mixture in as you go. Throw a few
thyme leaves and some extra cheese over the top, then bake for an
hour, until golden, sizzling and luxuriously indulgent.

Åsa's salmon with kale and sweet potato, for depression, seasonal affective disorder and low moods

Anyone who's ever suffered from depression – no matter how mild or short-lived – will know that it is stubborn. It comes to you and sticks like a burr. There's no banishing it with positive thinking or peppy mantras; no cocktail of anti-depressants can guarantee to lift the cloud away. But there are things that you can do to help yourself stay afloat through the sickness. There's one meal that I always turn to when my depression sets in: it's a meal that my friend Åsa made for me when I visited her in Norway, and it reminds me of all the joy I felt eating a dinner cooked for me by someone who cared. When I make it for myself now, it's a way of re-enacting that care, and showing myself the self-love I deserve. What's more, it's great for a sickly brain. It's a dish of baked salmon, served with kale and sweet potato mash. The salmon is high in omega 3 fatty acids, which are fantastic for brain function, and vitamin D, which can help to remedy the symptoms of seasonal affective disorder. Kale is a source of iron and potassium, while sweet potato provides a healthy dose of vitamin A, which is great for your skin and vision. And even without considering the vitamin- and mineral-rich credentials of the meal, it's a dish that makes you feel a little better just for the sheer vibrancy of it: bright green kale, pink salmon, terracotta sweet potatoes and a lot of good, home comfort.

To feed your body and soul with this perfect meal, first wrap the salmon fillets (one per eater) in little parcels of foil, rubbed with oil to prevent the fish sticking. Preheat the oven to 200°C/fan 180°C/gas mark 6, while you boil sweet potato chunks (roughly one medium-sized sweet potato per person) in plenty of salted water until soft. Roast the salmon parcels for up to 20 minutes, but check them often to make sure they don't overcook and sink into chalky dryness. For the last 5 minutes or so of the salmon's cooking time, put a fistful of kale per person – rubbed with olive oil and seasoned with plenty of sea salt flakes – on a separate tray into the oven to crisp and sizzle. Mash the sweet potato with butter, salt and – Åsa's secret ingredient – an extravagant drizzle of heavy cream.

Man-eaters

It's not just our bodies and physical needs that determine what we eat. There is a long history of people's diets being policed by parties far bigger than you or I. So many awful ideologies, no matter how lofty their ambitions, wiggle their toes in the mucky business of physical, tangible bodies. Women's feminine frames were once thought to have psychological weakness written into them; racism often finds a foothold in talk of bodies, sliding inexorably towards genetics, eugenics and more. The body is political. So it's not a huge leap to see how food – the very stuff that makes our bodies, drives us, and keeps us strong – is used to keep bodies, and the people within, in check.

Look, for instance, at Women Who Eat On Tubes. WWEOT is a Facebook group that rose to infamy in 2014. It functions as a platform for people to upload and disseminate fly-on-the-wall photos of unsuspecting women, well, eating on the Tube. There was some dialogue, at the time, about it being an artistic project, a witty glance at the nature of personhood today or some such. But at its heart it was, of course, about women's bodies, and what we do with those bodies. More specifically, it was about what claim others have to those bodies when we dare to live, eat and breathe in a public space. The man at the helm of the group, whom I won't name for fear of feeding his ego, shrugged the whole thing off in an interview with the *Telegraph*: 'They're in a public place. That's the risk that you take.' It's the risk you take, I guess, if you're not a man.

Maybe you're happy to just brush WWEOT off as a bit of a laugh, and that's fine. But it's worth looking at the ways in which these kinds of tiny 'jokes' take hold. They begin to sprout in the little comments in the office about what Debra or Lucy is having for lunch, and they reach up towards the sun on tiny, hopeful filaments as your boss points out that you ought to 'keep an eye on that belly, Anshima!' They lay their roots deeper with talk of women being prosecuted for what they eat and drink during pregnancy, and they pop open a thousand jubilant blossoms, like fireworks, with the onset of full, all-encompassing, diet culture. This is a diet culture that zooms its sordid little lens in on every lump and bump of women in the media, monetises weight loss and even pays celebrities to gain weight just so they can lose it all over again. To quote writer Lindy West from her book, *Shrill*: 'Society's monomaniacal fixation on female thinness isn't a distant abstraction, something to be pulled apart by academics in women's studies classrooms or leveraged for traffic in shallow "body-positive" listicles ... It is a constant, pervasive taint that warps every woman's life.'

It's a strange split: in our society, food and women are traditionally dismissed as frivolous, fanciful, feminine things, while also being the stuff of nightmares. As for the places where food and femininity intersect – lipsticked lips around full, chewing mouths; hen party tables sagging under the weight of rosé wine and penis lollipops – that's the scariest stuff of all. Think of snarling, hungry horror movie temptresses – childless old hags luring innocent brats into a forest with candy and cannibalistic cunning; vampire queens ensnaring the horny and hapless – it's no fun being a hungry woman. Witchcraft has particularly wicked and wonderful associations with food, as it happens: historians have noted the mirroring between witchy satanic feasts and their antithesis in the holy meals of the Eucharist. Some reports even have it that these ungodly feasts looked magical but, made with evil as they were, tasted like crap. From my limited experience of dinner parties, I can believe it.

Ultimately, we're terrified by the idea of women eating, being hungry, and getting healthier, heavier and happier. This is a world where the boundaries between consumption and self-denial, power and passivity often trace the crude line dividing men and women. Only men, and a terrifying Mia Farrow in horror classic *Rosemary's Baby*, eat rare steak. Yorkie bars are 'not for girls', which is just as well because they don't even taste good. We're told, in countless different ways, that we ought to be content with what we have, ask for less, take up less space. Where little boys tumble freely through childhood, all rambunctiousness and grazed knees, girls are encouraged to keep their elbows in and their voices down. Fat men are, to a degree, allowed to self-define as 'strapping young things'; fat women are 'overweight'.

Our appetite is only human, but that's just the thing: unless you're a man, those hungry, smelly, normal human things are taboo. Somehow, as women, we're expected to be superhuman – perfectly engineered, low-maintenance, minimalist machines for life – in exchange for the 'privilege' of being declared less-than by the society that spawned us. And these ideals have consequences. Up to 75% of eating disorder sufferers in the UK are women, according to the charity Anorexia & Bulimia Care. One 2016 study showed that 57% of UK women had tried to lose weight that year (compared with 48% of Brits in general). Clearly women's relationships with food are particularly conflicted, and the expectations heaped upon us – by a media saturated with images of idealised bodies, and by a pervasive culture of female guilt around food – only reinforce that confusion. When it comes to food, it's our gender that sets the standard, and most of the time it is women who pay the price.

Men aren't immune to these messages, though. In a study conducted by researchers at Aarhus University, it was found that women were happier to spend more money on 'healthy' foods after being exposed to pictures of good-looking men, and that men were quicker to blow the bank on pricey, prestige foods after seeing photos of attractive women. Clearly appetite isn't the only factor when it comes to choosing our food: we each have a whole vast web of beliefs, anxieties, morals and judgements that play into the decisions we make about what to eat. That expensive steak your date ordered could be a symbol of his virility, or a way to show that he's got money, or a nod to his masculinity. It could mean any one of the million subtexts that steak – and pretty much every other food under the sun – has been imbued with over time. Maybe it's a connection to his Argentinian heritage, or perhaps it's a statement in defiance of what he perceives to be 'wet' lefty vegetarianism. It could be an assertion of his hunger, and his desire to satisfy it no matter the cost. Maybe he's anaemic, maybe he's a gym freak. Maybe he just likes steak.

No type of appetite is exempt from these double standards. It's the same philosophy that allows men to be victorious stallions while women do the shambolic 3am 'walk of shame' after a one-night fling. Sexualities that diverge from the heterosexual mainstream are policed in a similar way (more on this in Bad taste, on page 160). It's why the female orgasm is shrouded in mystery even among grown women, while guys chat blithely about cum stains and luxury wanks. It's what makes women 'power-hungry' or 'manipulative' where men are 'ambitious' and 'shrewd'. If you fall outside the gender binary – even worse. Just the act of existing and asserting your non-binary gender in this world can be reframed as self-indulgent 'attention-seeking'. You're asking for too much just by *being*, apparently.

Gender politics might have moved on enough that it's no longer OK to explicitly demand the submission of women, but the sentiment hasn't gone away. Perhaps the cleverest thing our patriarchal society ever achieved was to rehash this bricks-and-mortar anti-woman rhetoric with something a hundred times more vague and harder to shoot down: now, instead of women's compliance being enforced as an imperative from above, it trickles down as a kind of pervasive doubt, finding a voice in the very women it keeps down. 'Am I too much?' we ask ourselves. 'Maybe if I were thinner/quieter/ sweeter, they'd like me more.' Dictates have given way to a culture of doubt. It's why my favourite advice column, *New York Magazine*'s 'Ask Polly', features some woman asking why she's 'too much' for guys more or less monthly. We've taken the rhetoric of our oppressors into our own mouths, and it's leaving a bitter taste.

I wish I could tell you to just shake off these toxic messages, let them sweep past you like a cooling breeze while you order your McFlurry and cheeseburger and text some guy for a quick hook-up. I wish we could all just ask for exactly what we want, when we want it, whether it's a back rub or a cheese fondue. I wish you could haul yourself to the top of the Empire State Building and fill your lungs with that smoky evening air and shout: 'I want a fucking girlfriend, OK?!' in the manner of Tom Hanks and Meg Ryan in *Sleepless in Seattle* (they don't say those exact words, true, but the feeling is there). But you can't just extricate yourself from a whole social, political system of ideologies just like that, through sheer force of will. These things take time, and there are moments where we all have to bow to convention and just order that salad without dressing instead of the three-dessert extravaganza we really want.

All we can really do is to take the revolution a meal at a time. Be the first woman in the office to take a biscuit from the communal tin; be the person brave enough to take the last one, too. In the company of people you feel comfortable with and safe around, eat your heart out. Practise ordering greedily on dates. Be the only person at the table to get a dessert. When it arrives, don't share it. Try out speaking your mind when you're alone – talk to yourself in the mirror, saying things like 'I would like you to go down on me, and I want the last slice of the strudel.' No doubt some people, probably guys, will be thrown off balance by your forthrightness. Who cares. Eat their leftovers. If they carry on judging you, eat them, too.

The F word

But, however frustrating I find the way that women are treated, I know I also have a huge advantage in being slim, in a society that is so brazenly unfair to fat people. It gives me the freedom to eat more freely, without fear. People may occasionally comment on my weight out of turn, or speculate on what's best for my health, but thinness affords me the luxury of being able to carry on; it means those comments don't materially hold me back. It's the reason that I've been able to carve out a niche for myself in the world of food writing, populated as it is so densely by thin women. Although all women's bodies are seen as public property, my slimness allows me to say 'follow your appetite' without someone hurling back at me: 'Look where that got you.' It means I can eat a burger safe in the knowledge that nobody will be raising an eyebrow, looking at my belly and unashamedly staring me down while connecting a whole load of dots that aren't necessarily connectable. Being this size allowed me to seek treatment for my eating disorder a few years ago, where a bigger person's experience might have been invalidated with a chorus of 'you're not *really* ill though, are you?'

There are infinite ways that a body can look, feel, take up space in the world, be desired, love and be loved. Every body – able, disabled, athletic, soft, tall, short – contains the whole universe within it. Fat bodies are no exception. I have friends who have that infinity drawn on their skin, adorning their fat bodies with tattooed constellations of food, people, stars, flora and fauna. I know other people who, in defiance of the high street fashion's size 18 ceiling, cloak themselves in tulle, satin and velvet, condensing the vastness of a whole century of fashion and exalting it on one fat body. And in spite of all of this, 'fat' has become shorthand for 'bad'. And with the shrinking of that word, so fat people are expected to shrink themselves.

To return again to the writings of Lindy West (who is as eloquent on matters of fatness as she is on feminism):

> I got good at being small early on – socially, if not physi-
> cally. In public, until I was eight, I would speak only to
> my mother, and even then only in whispers, pressing my
> face into her leg. I retreated into fantasy novels, movies,
> computer games and, eventually, comedy – places where I
> could feel safe, assume any personality, fit into any space.

Another facet of this enforced shrinking is that those with fat bodies are deemed somehow incapable of knowing what is best for them. Their health is picked over and diets dissected under the somewhat fanatically fat-obsessed lens of the media. I'm wary of adding to that chorus of preaching voices, which is why I asked my friend Bethany Rutter, a self-proclaimed rad fat babe who has written extensively about her experience as a fat woman, what one thing most affects her life, when it comes to food and fatness. She told me:

> I wish people understood better the genuine fear that can
> come with eating in public while fat … Sure, people who
> aren't fat probably have some anxiety about eating alone,
> or ending up with tomato sauce on their face and not
> knowing about it, but the fear of stares, whispers, judge-
> ment or even *actual harassment* that comes with being fat
> and eating, especially alone, is next level. I like hanging
> out in McDonald's on my own when I have time to kill:

it's inside, I can sit down and read something, it's cheap etc. But every time I do, I think 'am I going to get harassed as a lone fat woman? Am I fair game because I'm playing up to a stereotype?' Understand: this fear is rooted in experience.

The harassment doesn't stop with food. People with fat bodies are humiliated on planes and public transport, where seats are refused to them. Artist Stacy Bias created a six-minute animation called *Flying While Fat*, about the ways in which fat bodies are scrutinised and vilified on planes, where their very presence is resented. Those deemed to be overweight are routinely refused medical care unless they lose weight, regardless of whether their illness is related to their size. My fat friends struggle to find clothes on the high street, and have even been photographed, filmed or laughed at just for having the audacity to exist in public. In an essay for *The New York Times*, writer Taffy Brodesser-Akner described attending a Weight Watchers meeting at which she 'celebrated' the 25th anniversary of her first ever diet. Fatphobia – that is, prejudice directed towards fat people – is one of the most enduringly 'acceptable' forms of discrimination in our society. Most of us know by now that you shouldn't use slurs against gay people, for instance (although that's certainly not to say that we don't still perpetuate these oppressions in other, less conspicuous, insidious ways, and society's acceptance does not yet extend equally to everybody in the LGBTQ+ family). But when it comes to fatphobia, it's no holds barred.

There will be those who try to frame our society's hatred of fatness as a benevolent mission. These people say they are just concerned for the well-being of their fat friends and family, while themselves smoking forty cigarettes a day. Between sips of their third can of Red Bull that day, they confess that they're worried about their fat friend becoming diabetic. 'It's just that she doesn't seem happy,' they say, while putting their loved one on a lettuce-and-carrot-sticks diet. The extreme sports fanatic, who has broken various bones twenty times, is worried about the strain that obesity is allegedly putting on the NHS. Thinness just isn't a guarantee of health. A 'perfect' BMI doesn't stand for anything if you've achieved it by thirty years of yo-yo dieting. Fitting into size 8 jeans won't help you if you're knocking back a brewery every night after work. Being slim is not, should never be, the gold standard. This facade of caring is pretty flimsy.

The snaky duplicity of anti-fat crusaders even hits to the liberatory efforts of fat activism. Just as my friend Bethany is accused of 'glorifying obesity' just for having the gumption to exist without shame, Lindy describes being harangued with the same question – 'isn't this a slippery slope into poor health?' – every time she asserts her humanity as a fat woman. As she puts it: 'The question itself is an assault: it validates the idea that fat people's humanity is one side of a debate, that our bodies are public property.'

There are studies linking high BMI to heart disease and diabetes, sure. But there are also studies which suggest that people classed as overweight have *longer* life expectancies and reduced susceptibility to certain diseases. The truth is complex and knotty. But regardless of whatever health imperatives eventually turn out to be right or wrong, it doesn't change the right of all people to fair, respectful treatment. These things are not privileges to be earned upon completion of some yellow-brick-road weight-loss journey. There is no magic cure or salve to fend off the intractable march of death: the diet industry wizard is a whole load of hot air. What is clear, when the enormity of life and death is reduced to a question of thinness and fatness, is that it's not really about health at all. Those of us who are slim ought to stop projecting our own neuroses about illness and mortality onto bodies that differ from ours. We need to cast off that one false fat–thin, bad–good dichotomy. Most of all, we need to mind our own damn business.

And those of us who are not thin – who are plus-size, fat, curvy, chubby and everything in between – it's not my place to tell you what to think or feel or eat or do. It is difficult to exist as a fat person in a determinedly thin world. But I want to just share this, written by Bethany for a mental health zine we once worked on together:

> When all around you are messages that certain things are not for you, it's hard to figure out how to live. A good place to start is to think about what you would want from life if you weren't constantly told that your experience is limited by your fat body. Who would you ask out on a date? How would you dress? Would you want to do a certain kind of exercise? Imagining these possibilities is the first step to building the confidence to live that life in practice.

Fed up

To hell with toeing the line. Our bodies are magical things. We go through our lives taking little bits of the world into us, bite by bite, and turning all of that matter into *us*. We get bigger, stronger, brighter, bolder, taking up more space – asserting the primacy of our existence – with every morsel we eat. Fat bodies are big and perfect, and deserve plates of meatballs made with the most tender care. Thin bodies are small and lithe – feed them until their bellies swell strange and round against their little frames. Women's bodies need big dishes of hearty protein, so they can flex their guns and store that extra fat on their stomachs and hips. Give elegant macaroons and éclairs and daintily iced biscuits to men, and fill their bodies with sweetness. For the non-binary people around you, serve crumpets dripping with butter to stoke the fires of their souls. Smother disabled bodies with the love of a perfectly ripe nectarine in the summer sun, a wedge of birthday cake or the final Rolo in the packet. Flood children with all the dazzling flavours of peanut butter, licked straight from a finger, scoops of cake batter, sizzling bacon rashers. Nourish yourself as though you're taking care of the most precious thing in the world: strengthen your bones with milkshakes, patch up cuts and bruises with cheese on toast. Eat for your life.

Digested: Eating with the seasons

It is spring, and the world is creaking into life. The trees shrug off their winter ache, arching their boughs and flushing green with tender new leaves. The ground begins to stir with new life, and every shoot, bird and bug scurries into action, laying the groundwork for a summer glut. This is a wonderful time to start thinking about eating seasonally, because this big spring awakening is already all about newness, growth and change. The more gracefully you can yield to the seasons' wax and wane, the more firmly you'll plant your feet on the ground and feel part of this world, this place, in this moment. Eating seasonally is about being present – weaving yourself into the earth you inhabit.

Around March or April each year, our soils offer up a momentous harvest. From the heavy clay earth of estuary Essex to the shattered crests of the Peaks, something is blooming. Shops with their foundations deep in the British ground start to blossom, an energy swelling up through the ground and rippling through the floor and culminating in a technicolour bounty that unfurls in shades of purple, gold, red and silver. Everywhere you turn, there are Easter eggs of every conceivable shape and size: huge hollow eggs that rattle with Smarties, heavy little Creme Eggs like lucky charms. There are strange fruits – chocolate bunnies and ducks and chicks – and precious speckled seeds – Mini Eggs in crisp sugar shells. This magic comes flooding the supermarkets for just a few weeks each year, disappearing as quickly as it came. If you want to feel at one with the rhythms of the world, this is a good place to start.

By the time the final shards of chocolate egg have been eaten, the summer is almost here, creeping in on a soft spring-time breeze. Cool mornings coax into warm days, and a cherry blossom blush carpets the pavements. The sensations of summer are fuzzy-stemmed tomatoes plump with juice, and the polished crimson skins of a punnet of cherries. There are fragrant peaches and ears of corn and tiny peas. The sunshine tastes like the strawberries that cascade from their straw-lined beds as June draws to a close. But not all the flavours of summer are as pure. It also tastes of a Twister ice lolly – packaged some place far away, a long time ago, but seasonally hand-picked from the corner shop freezer – and funfair bales of candy floss. This is the season of last-minute supermarket visits, swinging by in the car with the windows down and Lorde crooning from the sound system, the whole town unexpectedly brought together in the Tesco car park in search of chicken wings and barbecue lights on an uncharacteristically sun-drenched day. It's a time for garnishing meals with stray lawn trimmings and flying ants, batting wasps away from Fanta bottles and downing a lukewarm Red Stripe on a damp little patch of grass in the park. While you still can, make sure you catch that most elusive of summer delicacies: the vanilla soft-serve ice cream cone, straight from the ice cream van.

Whenever I read Nigel Slater's Kitchen Diaries, *I'm taken in by a fantasy of autumn that's seasoned with pumpkin, sausage, sweet brown onions and thyme. He describes a quiet September and reverent October, sacred moments of harvest-time splendour decked out in copper, amber and gold, seized before the cold kiss of winter arrives. My autumn doesn't look like this. So bereft am I that another summer has passed me by without me really capitalising on it, I spend much of autumn's opening scenes knocking back Pimm's and making salads with hard, sour out-of-season fruits. Clawing back precious time from the encroaching dark evenings, I fall into the familiar comfort of ready meals and one-pot dinners and, when the autumn glut of blockbuster food books arrives on the shelves just in time for a Christmas splurge, I gorge myself on these, too. I drink up the perfect food porn and the lavish descriptions of meals I'll never eat. I sip on my Pumpkin Spice Latte and I give thanks for the harvest.*

The whole of the rest of the year is, of course, just a count-down to Christmas. The fuss starts sometime around October and the fervour mounts day by day until, by the end of December, we're so thoroughly sick of it all that just the sight of a mince pie is enough to break a family apart. This is a magical time for eating, though. Mother nature may close shop before the big freeze, but retailers come into their own. Supermarkets become wonderlands filled with favourites we'd almost forgotten (brandy! shortbread! yule log!) and favourites we never knew we had (mince pie flavour ice cream! toffee apple cider!). Every mangled novelty food you could ever have dreamed of comes hurtling onto the shelves, from mulled wine jellies to Christmas cronuts. Winter brings out the cynics and the nay-sayers, bemoaning the death of the humble yuletide and so on, which is why it's only right to throw yourself headlong into the madness and eat every weird and wonderful ostentatious sea-sonal delight you can.

It won't be long before the fog clears and the new year hurtles into view with all its promises of a 'new year, new you', diets and fresh starts. But the thing about the seasons is that they are cyclical, and the 'new you' this January will be the same 'new you' of next January, and of every January until you die. You'll drift from Creme Egg spring to Red Stripe summer and

Pumpkin Spice autumn and right back to the fugue state you started in, dizzy from all the brandy butter, nursing a hangover in a bed. Maybe that's all part of the march of the seasons, though. We drift through hope and hunger with the whims of the seasons, and embed ourselves in the communities we live in by yielding to a shared culinary calendar. Maybe sometime in the distant past we had to bend to the whims of nature, but now most of us live in places where strawberries fill the shelves the whole year round, and in the flood of orange streetlamps, the night is as bright as the day. We take our cues not from the sun or the stars or the earth but from the societies that nurture us. We plough the supermarkets and pick the crisps and wake early to take in the healing morning coffee. Every day is a feast.

You are what you eat?

A tale of two caterpillars

It is spring in the American South-West. From Arizona to the verdant, crumpled landscape of western Texas, the oak trees are beginning to bloom, erupting in firework tendrils of knobbly yellow-green catkins, bobbing and quivering in the lazy breeze, little sunbursts dripping from the thick green foliage of the stunted desert oak. It isn't easy to see, but look closely enough at this normal tree, on a normal spring day, and mischief begins to stir among its leaves. Fix your eyes on the rustlings of the golden catkins and you might see, festooned in knobbly yellow-green 'buds' of its own, a very hungry caterpillar.

This caterpillar is the larva of the *Nemoria arizonaria* moth. It emerges in spring, and feasts upon the oak catkins, cleverly disguised thanks to the yellow-ish little flower bud shapes that cluster along the length of its back and belly. It looks, to predators, or you, or I, exactly like a golden spring catkin.

As spring flattens under the encroaching summer heat, the caterpillar hides away, becomes a pupa, and eventually emerges as a moth – leaf green, with light 'veins' threaded across its fuzz-edged wings. It vanishes among the leaves without a trace. And then autumn comes. What you might expect, when the eggs laid by the summer moths start hatching, is a new tangle of yellow-green catkin caterpillars. But there's a twist in the tale.

By the time the summer has faded and this second generation of caterpillars has come into the world, the oak's spring catkins have long gone. The tree is heavy with grey-green leaves. A caterpillar coiffed to within an inch of its life in shades of chartreuse, decked out with bells and whistles, would never survive in this monochrome world. So it doesn't try. These autumn caterpillars grow fuzzy, a greenish grey, slim and twig-like. They forge themselves in the image of the sticks and shoots they live among. But just how could these two caterpillars – a single generation apart, and genetically identical – look so different?

'Caterpillar Disguise: You Are What You Eat' is the title of a 1989 article in the journal *Science News*. Speaking to the journal, researcher Erick Greene of the University of California hypothesised that the eventual form of the caterpillars is dependent on the levels of tannins in the food they consume. The spring catkins are low in tannins, and spring-born caterpillars react to this by very quickly growing into their catkin coats. In autumn on the other hand, with the catkins gone and the leaves rich with tannins, the caterpillars' bodies receive a different cue. This cue sets off something in them that makes them grow green, streamlined and stick-like, just like the environment they live in. Eat catkins, become 'catkins'. Eat leaves and shoots, become woody little 'twigs'. Nestled among the branches of just another oak tree, live many tiny, wriggling, hungry embodiments of the time-old adage that you are what you eat.

Caterpillars are particularly potent symbols when it comes to food. They eat and eat and eat and eat, then hole themselves up in a chrysalis and emerge either as a beautiful lace-winged butterfly, or a moth. In this one metamorphosis, all of the power of food plays out: one heavy, sluggish little body becomes – with the help of a raging appetite and the whole of nature's bounty at its disposal – a soaring, delicate thing.

Eric Carle wrote about this appetite, and where it leads, in his 1969 classic *The Very Hungry Caterpillar*, some twenty years before Greene discovered the secrets of the emerald *Nemoria arizonaria* moth. The very hungry caterpillar eats one piece of chocolate cake, one ice cream cone, one pickle, one slice of Swiss cheese, and one slice of salami. He gnaws through an apple and a piece of cherry pie and a cupcake. He gorges on a lollipop and two pears and a slice of watermelon, and rolls blearily into a chrysalis to sleep off the stomach ache. When he emerges, he is every single colour under the rainbow, and he spreads his wings, and flies.

It was French food writer Jean Anthelme Brillat-Savarin who famously wrote '*dis-moi ce que tu manges, je te dirai ce que tu es*' – 'tell me what you eat, I will tell you what you are' – and with this put into words the whole essence of the 'you are what you eat' philosophy. This logic is what drives us when we peer into other people's supermarket trolleys, making checkout Inspector Clouseaus of us all. It drives the entire diet and wellness industry and forms the basis for a whole barrage of toxic ideology around food. It makes girls from sugar and spice, magicking sweetness from sweets. It's the thinking behind the hackneyed claim that fatty food makes you fat, or that eating lots of red meat will give you big biceps.

Food obviously doesn't work quite as literally as that, but the heart of the idea still rings true. We're strange composites of all the food we put in our mouths. Every strand of your hair, every perfect, swelling belly roll, is made of thin-crust pizza, gummy bears and pineapple so sweet-sharp it stings the roof of your mouth. Your toes are sausages, your teeth are made of milk and honey. Each bite and sip fills our bellies with the raw ingredients to cook up a whole human body.

Turtles and boars

There's a simplistic way to look at this business of eating: what's important is *stuff*. To be made of peas, Doritos and strawberry laces is to be physically, atomically made of those things. Every mouthful digested means a million tiny molecules of goodness (or not) flooding your gut, and flowing through your veins. Calcium from the milk on your Coco Pops helps build your bones, vitamin A from the carrots in your lunchbox makes your eyes strong. This is the kind of 'you are what you eat' that forms the foundations of nutritional science and (more on this later) the diet industry. But there's a lot more to eating and absorption and metamorphosis than just the processes that happen under the lens of the microscope. As rational and clever as we think we are, our ideas around food are, more often than not, the result of magical thinking: much as we might think we are carefully weighing the vitamin content of one menu option against another, more often we're making decisions based on our sense of what particular foods *represent*.

A 1989 study divided participants into two groups, then asked each group to read slightly different statements about the diets of a fictional tribe. The first group read that the tribe commonly ate boar, while the second group was told that the tribe's diet centred on turtle meat. These participants weren't nutritionists – they knew nothing about the nutritional value of turtle or boar, or what nutrients those things might contain – and with this in mind, you wouldn't expect them to be able to say much at all about the health, character or lifestyle of the tribespeople. But they had a *lot* to say. The boar-eaters were, apparently, heavy-set and good at running. The turtle-eaters were strong swimmers and long-lived. Each group had taken what they knew about boars and turtles and transcribed those traits onto the people of the tribe, as though these characteristics could pass from prey, to stomach, to blood, to the very essence of the eater.

This kind of thinking has been around since antiquity, evolving from Galen's medical theories in the Roman Empire to the beliefs of philosopher and physician Paracelsus in the sixteenth century. According to the latter, 'Nature marks each growth ... according to its curative benefit.' The whole world was, for Paracelsus, kindly signposted by God, with nature's remedies created in the image of the parts of us that they can cure. Saxifrage fractured rocks with its roots so should be used to treat kidney stones. Bloodwort seeped reddish sap, and so could heal disorders of the blood.

If all this sounds irrational, just look at the rhetoric built up around the food that we eat every day. I notice myself peering into other people's shopping trolleys a lot. Whenever I was dragged to the supermarket as a kid, my mum and dad would be dissecting the state of other people's shopping as soon as we had left the checkout. The man in front of us in the queue had £40 worth of cat food, a beef hotpot meal and a packet of rich tea biscuits: 'a real loner' my mum would say. The family behind us, my dad would add, had that Alpen muesli, and the gold-top milk, and the carrots with the frilly bits still on, and mum might nod sagely and roll her eyes.

We are judged by what we put in our baskets. The idea is that you can tell a lot about a person by the food they buy; each receipt is like a through-the-keyhole insight into the indulgences and idiosyncrasies of someone's life. With that in mind, I've started curating my shopping basket with a kind of pathological vanity that has surprised even me: slipping the Haribo and the tampons to the bottom, and arranging the herbs, fresh fish and fancy chocolate on top. This basket says: 'I am a functioning adult; I am good at food and therefore good at life.' This is the person I want to appear to be.

This literalism is the basis of a hugely profitable chunk

of our contemporary food culture. Through the 1980s and 90s, the weight-loss business was built on the mantra 'eat fat, get fat'. A whole generation ate grapefruit and black coffee for breakfast, painstakingly cut the fat off their bacon, and dined on grilled chicken breast with the succulence of an old boot. Today, the emphasis has changed but the feeling remains the same: eat 'heavy' (salty, fatty, carby) meals, and you will feel heavy in body and soul. Greasy food makes a greasy person – a pizza diet will give you a 'pizza face', blocking your pores and leaving you glistening with oil. When we describe someone as 'white bread' or 'vanilla', we're extrapolating personalities from beige foods, we're relying on some vague faith that like begets like, and that what we eat will show in who we are.

By the 'you are what you eat' logic, junk food makes for junk people, and unfamiliar food makes for strange, 'different' people. It's worth questioning the assumptions we make about what's normal, plain, right or good in food, and what's not. Often, these judgements we make about food and identity say much more about the person airing them than they do about the people doing the eating.

Within Western Europe and much of North America, where whiteness is seen as default, 'plain' foods can come to stand for the status quo, and even the enforcement of that status quo. What could be more all-American than the naked pallor of a Thanksgiving turkey, or the bland sweetness of apple pie? It might even be accompanied with a scoop of vanilla ice cream or custard, the supposed baseline flavour from which all other varieties 'diverge'.

Conversely, the food of 'outsiders' is marked by its otherness. Take the 'good, honest' heft of a steaming, greasy parcel of fish and chips, compared with the 'frilliness' of traditional French cuisine. I read a review on Amazon once of a truly great Ghanaian cookbook, where the reviewer described

Ghanaian food as 'visually unappealing and based around starchy, tasteless root vegetables', as though British food were a platter of technicolour delights and not a grey meditation on gammon and egg and potatoes. Every kid who ever got laughed at for their 'weird', 'smelly' packed lunch will know what I mean when I say that the unknown – specifically the edible unknown – terrifies people. A lunchbox of *tabbouleh* or *adobo* is as sensational as a flying saucer.

It is, of course, understandable that the foods we are brought up with sit at the centre of our food world. They give us a familiar reference point, an edible blueprint for understanding food. When I think of bread, for instance, I think of a loaf of featherweight sliced white. Someone else, at a different time, in a different place, might think of burnished twisted loaves of challah, nutty rye bread, or crisp, sweet *pandesal*. In Japan, rice is so integral to the national diet that the word *gohan*, or 'rice', can be used to refer to a 'meal' more generally. 'Breakfast' can even be translated as *asagohan*, or 'morning rice'.

Where many of us trip up, though, is falling back on time-old racist tropes to make sense of these cultural differences. A 1903 article in *The New York Times* alleged that the Tupinambá people, of the Tupi ethnic group in the Brazilian Amazon, 'take on simian and arboreal attributes and become as thievish and chattering as the animals [they] consume'. More recently, a Kent landlord instructed agents not to let his properties to people of colour because the smell of curry 'sticks to the carpet'. White supremacists drink milk as a cultural emblem of, and a visual symbol of, a mythic 'pure' whiteness. When we unquestioningly accept Western European and American food as a default, we risk not only overlooking all the incredible diversity of food in Britain today, but also tarring people who eat 'foreign' food with the same brush of 'otherness' that we use to define the food itself.

On the other hand, there are the supposed mystical healing powers of so-called superfoods: goji berries, chia seeds, acai – all rising above the stolid, everyday kind of nutrition that home-grown produce can offer. These 'superfoods', despite having been thoroughly debunked (they're just foods! with vitamins and antioxidants and other good things in! like more or less every other food!), perpetuate the myth that if you spend enough, and buy foods from all four corners of the globe, you can cheat death. These foods are the edible equivalent of the 'magical' black character trope in film and TV – a 'strange', 'mystical' outsider, helping the white person to fulfil their destiny. Think Whoopi Goldberg's character in *Ghost*, or Michael Clarke Duncan in *The Green Mile*. These exotic superfoods, too, are picked up as quickly as they're cast off. They fit into a pretty long and established tradition of white people grabbing hold of symbols of otherness while it suits them, and quickly letting go as soon as fortunes or fashions change.

Either way, whether traditional British foods are seen as comforting 'real food' or condemned for their boring familiarity, we too often see them as a kind of starting point, a normal that forms the counterpoint to an exotic, spicy, strange 'other'.

To see a world in a tub of poo

In the TV series *You Are What You Eat*, first broadcast in 2004, the nation looked on aghast as presenter 'Dr' Gillian McKeith told people that they looked haggard, and then poked at samples of their poo in Tupperware boxes to assess exactly how haggard they were and why. McKeith took Brillat-Savarin's 200-year-old observation with a literalism that nobody could've predicted, prompting a whole generation to measure their worth not by how much fun they had, or how kind they were, but by the finer details of their poo.

There's obviously some logic to the spectacle: it can tell us a lot about what's going on inside of us, and how we could do better. These kind of unsavoury poo clues can even save lives, if we look closely. Black stools can be a sign of internal bleeding, while very pale poo can mean that fat isn't being digested as it should be – a sign of coeliac disease. But these are conclusions that should be drawn by a doctor, and confirmed by tests.

Aside from the questionable ethics of subjecting people to these poo inspections and colonic irrigations on national TV, where McKeith really fell into murky waters was in the attitude she took towards these 'patients'. She read the stool like a set of tarot cards, and with all the grace of a fortune teller on Southend seafront, declared the person doomed if they continued to live the way they were. To one victim, McKeith declared: 'You don't deserve to have a body.' This wasn't a medical professional making measured diagnoses from study, examination and careful consideration, this was a cruel and wayward shill measuring the whole of a person by the quality of their smelliest moments.

In 2007, the Advertising Standards Authority asked McKeith to desist from promoting herself as a doctor in her books and television shows, while physician and writer Ben Goldacre exposed the nullity of her 'doctor' qualification by buying a similar title from the American Association of Nutritional Consultants and bestowing it on his dead cat. Following the controversy, McKeith's career slowly wound up where it had begun: in shit.

Her legacy lives on, though, in the slew of aggressively intrusive food exposé shows that fill our TV screens even today. These shows aren't quite the same as they were in McKeith's heyday: at some point during the late noughties, public sensibilities wavered and we collectively decided that maybe it wasn't OK to flat-out tell people they were revolting on primetime TV. If *You Are What You Eat* was the weight-loss equivalent of sending deserving adults head-first into a gunge tank, this new generation of fat-shaming programming took a more circuitous route towards redemption. The weight-loss imperative became cloaked in faux concern for health, encouraging participants to 'regain their confidence' or 'gain energy' by – surprise surprise – losing weight. But still, just like McKeith's cruel-to-be-kind methodology that came before, shows like *Supersize vs Superskinny* and *Secret Eaters* shocked guests into lifestyle overhauls by presenting, with a flourish, tables heaped with all the food they'd eaten, canisters filled high with chips and beans, blocks of lard acting as visual metaphors for the fat these guests had filled their bodies with that week. It's a format designed to shock, but above all, to shame: in *Secret Eaters*, participants are made to say, through their tears, 'I am a secret eater', while the presenter and resident dietitian look on with beneficent pride.

What every one of these shows preaches is that a terrible diet makes a terrible person, and that that terribleness will end up writ large in your pimply skin and dull hair and bad personality. It's just what we do when we peer over those little checkout divider bars and read laziness, unloveability, fecklessness, wastefulness or greed into the foods on the conveyor in front of us. Our judgement is far-reaching: you are what you eat, and what you eat is bad.

The strangest thing about all these moral judgements is the aura of scientific certainty in which they are cloaked. Every food packet has calorie information, data on the grams and milligrams and micrograms of every vitamin and mineral you've never heard of. We know exactly how much saturated fat there is in our Twix, and precisely how many teaspoons of sugar is the maximum we should consume every day. Our diets are cut into neat numerical bites, and we put our faith in these numbers with a kind of religious fervour. And yet in spite of all this data, we have some decidedly magical ways of conceptualising food. 'Clean' diets lead to a trouble-free life, 'pure' foods give the eater a clarity of thinking, a wellness-driven lifestyle will smooth out the snags in your world. This belief system centres on the idea that a perfect diet – clear rules, no muddying of ingredients, no heaviness, no poison, no muck – will in turn give your life those same clean lines, boundaries and simplicity.

Food writers, bloggers and presenters cleverly make pasta from courgettes, rice from cauliflower, meat from carrot, all in an attempt to avoid the 'heaviness' of meat and carbs, and so to keep their bodies light and lithe. They talk about bloating, head fog, sluggishness and weight, and plant the seed that these feelings are the symptoms of a bloaty, muddled, slothful diet. The 'bowl' trend of 2016 (put a bunch of ingredients in a bowl and call it a marvel meal) sums up the weird superstitious energy prevalent in food at the moment: separate ingredients, prepared individually, and all portioned neatly in a bowl stand in stark contrast to the integral messiness of curry and rice, or pasta and sauce. This is an era of nervousness, a fear of mixing and uncertainty, a need to know exactly what's on your plate and, presumably, exactly how many calories it contains. How the hell did things get this way?

Eat me, drink me

To get to the heart of wellness, we actually have to shuffle away from the sterile, minimalist, millennial apartments in which it was forged, towards something way bigger than just diets or gluten or superfoods. As much as it tries to float free of heavy, human things, the roots of wellness burrow deep into the fertile soil of graveyards; they twist down through church spires, tumble across altars and into chalices and push hellwards through the heavy flagstone floors. The real essence of wellness burns steady in the damp air, the dimness and the weight of religion.

Health and faith have been bound together for as long as we've walked this earth with aches and pains and illness, from Jesus healing the blind to the healing scriptures of the Qur'an – 'Mankind there has come to you a guidance from your Lord and a healing for [the diseases] in your hearts, and for those who believe a guidance and a mercy.' In Judaism, a focus on wholeness, or *shleimut*, gives rise to a view of an interconnected spiritual, mental and physical self, far from the fractured view of humanity that scientific medicine might lead us to, while in a 1627 recipe book, Elizabeth Bulkeley provides a 'recipe' called 'A speciall meanes to preserve health', instructing the reader to 'rise from syn willinglie' and 'take vp Christes Crosse boudlie'. She's no Delia, but clearly matters of bodily health and spiritual well-being have always shared common ground.

It wasn't until the sixteenth century that anatomist Vesalius literally and figuratively dissected these old belief systems about the body. Authoring anatomical manual *De humani corporis fabrica*, Vesalius peeled back skin, showed limber skeletons striking a pose, and gave us a peek at the stuff we're made of, guts and all. Another 300 years passed until modern medicine, as we'd recognise it today, really began to bloom. In the space of a short fifteen years in the mid-1800s, physicians developed anaesthesia, antisepsis, and the first theories about cells, microbes and all the nitty-gritty that makes us work. When holistic, faith-based medicine has moulded our view of personhood for so long, it's little wonder that wellness harks back to that way of thinking. Modern medicine is relatively new and, in spite of our devotion to our clergy of doctors and liturgy of pills, it's hard not to feel the tug of the divine and the allure of the vague, and tumble right back into spiritual visions of health. Whenever you see ancient grains, whole foods, traditional remedies and ayurvedic healing in the brightly lit aisles of Holland and Barrett, it's that feeling that's being marketed to you.

This quasi-religious impulse comes through tellingly in the rituals of wellness. The church walls carry the stations of the cross, and the sermons fall into well-worn ruts of the sermon, prayer and scripture. There is a considered deliberation to everything that happens, and even the smallest act is cloaked in ceremony, from the altar cloth to the catechism. In the same way, there's a real fussiness to wellness that follows these familiar rhythms: smoothie bowls with fruit arranged on top just so, carefully layered noodle jars, mindful eating, and the intricacies of table setting. This is the inversion of unscripted, rapturous, messy meals. The devil is in the detail.

Even the vocabulary of the church of wellness borrows from sermon. Look into diet plans, wellness cookbooks and clean living tutorials, and you find good and evil, miracles, cures, healing, hope, bright new futures and promised salvation. Between every line, seasoning every recipe, is the implied promise of eternal life. Weight-loss industry behemoth Slimming World uses not calories but 'syns' to measure food intake, with 'syn' supposedly short for 'synergy' and not just a baseless allusion to moral sin. The early noughties M&S advert-inspired rhetoric of indulgence, decadence and hedonism has been swept away in recent years, in favour of its converse: a diet that values lightness, cleanness and goodness. The founders of certain controversial diets even imply that babies can be born unhealthy – the wellness of their digestive systems screwed from the outset – while promising redemption in a grain-free, legume-free, high-kale diet. This kind of damnation and carrot-on-a-stick salvation looks a lot like original sin to me.

This food subculture is riddled with healing miracles, too.

I see your Jesus healing the blind, and I raise you. Ella Mills (aka Deliciously Ella) and her postural tachycardia, the symptoms of which 'all but disappeared' with the help of a vegan diet. Look at Belle Gibson, the wellness blogger who famously faked an inoperable brain tumour, which she then 'healed' through a diet that she went on to make a great deal of money from. Once they've run their course, there's nothing particularly divine about these stories: a romantic urban myth about purity and healing, turned sour in the cold light of day. One wellness personality, Jessica Ainscough, even died from her untreated cancer, which she claimed she could heal 'naturally' through diet and lifestyle. But it's not really evidence or results that matter in questions of faith: it's the promises that sell. And wellness is ripe with promises.

What wellness culture asserts, in essence, is that there is some higher state we can achieve, but only if we're willing to put in the work. Our natural impulses, the ones that draw us to the buzz of sugar, the sting of salt, bright sweets and festive feasts, are all wrong according to the wellness mantra. The way to upper-middle-class white-girl heaven? You gotta get there through chia seeds, suppressing all your natural urges, and yoga.

Ultimately, it's not even the food itself that sells these diets. Most of the power of these miracle regimes is bound up in the bodies that endorse them – the celebrities and influencers who use their overwhelmingly privileged, slim, white, attractive bodies to advertise the food that made those bodies. These 'desirable' bodies are supposed to be the blemish-free result of an everything-free diet, and we buy into the mystical fantasy that if we eat that way, then we, too, might have lustrous hair, an apartment in Chelsea and razor-sharp abs.

These young women are rich, thin and toned, and we want what they have. So we eat up images of their bodies, just as we eat up the foods they sell. We wash down our acai bowl with thinspiration, and this ascetic meal cleanses us of our bodily guilt, and nudges us one step closer to immortality. Just as the eucharist gives Catholics a piece of bread that's Christ's body, and the wine that's Christ's blood, so we consume the bodies and blood of the leaders of the wellness movement. We eat what they eat, and in turn we eat them, and we save our wretched souls. For all the faith we have in evidence and numbers, the success of wellness comes down to plain, unscientific hope.

The same old you

None of this is to say that the individual ingredients or techniques that wellness espouses are harmful. I'm sure there are elements of this new health-driven movement that are even good. The shift away from crash dieting, for instance (an incredible 97% of dieters regain their lost weight, and then some, within three years), is a good thing, although the movement as a whole remains as violently fatphobic as ever. It is probably good to have more vegetables on your plate. Maybe acai berries deserve the superfood title, but if not, they probably aren't doing you any harm either.

And yet, no matter what little things wellness can deliver on, it will always fall short on its promise of redemption. There is no way to streamline your body for maximal efficiency. You can't live for ever, and there's not a diet under the sun that will safeguard you from disease. There's no reinvention through carb-cutting. You think Beyoncé sat down before making *Lemonade* and thought to herself, 'I know what will make this the single most important contribution to pop music in a decade – I'll make sure I activate my grains before I eat them'? I think not. The fundamental tenet of wellness is that it can make you into a better, happier, healthier person. As a diet that moralises and prescribes, and encourages cutting out some of the most important and culturally significant foods we have, I'd say it fails.

The thing is, we are always who we are. I have been around the block a hundred thousand times when it comes to reinvention. I have dyed, cut, shaved and straightened my hair. I have Googled 'how to disappear without a trace' with a straight face, and started weightlifting, climbing, running and swimming in turn, at every low ebb in my life. I've dressed in high camp pink velvet, and gone out in what felt like drag, in tight tops, short skirts and even a pair of five-inch stiletto silver glitter boots. I have gone vegetarian and vegan and omnivorous. I've slipped into eating disorders under the weight of my panicked need just to be different, even if being different meant not being at all. When diet is such an integral part of our identity, it's easy to succumb to the tempting idea that you can reinvent, resurrect and evolve simply by going on a diet. But it just doesn't work that way.

All those bristly, uncomfortable, short-tempered, imperfect, morally questionable bits of you are who you are, and they're swirled through the muddle of goodness and badness at the core of your soul. You are strange, wobbly, angular, lazy, stressy. You're going to spend your whole life trying to pick apart these threads and make sense of this absolute chaos of contradictions – we all are. You're going to wonder how the hell you get anything done when the heart of who you are is just one big 'WHY?'. And all of this is OK, because life is confusing and strange and often unhappy, and there's no diet that can gloss over this. No perfectly choreographed parade of little vegetable nibbles or energy balls can cure that feeling inside of you, because you know what? There's nothing to cure. That absolute mess is an abstract painting, and nobody understands what on earth it means, but it is perfect and it is you.

Rich and smoky bean stew

Fry three crushed cloves of garlic in a large saucepan with a couple of tablespoons of vegetable oil. When golden, add three tablespoons of tomato ketchup, a teaspoon of wholegrain mustard, a heaped teaspoon of smoked paprika, a quarter to a half of a teaspoon of cayenne and a quarter of a teaspoon of cinnamon. Cook for a minute over a medium–low heat before adding a tin of chopped tomatoes, two drained tins of borlotti, haricot, pinto, red kidney or butter beans, and a chicken or vegetable stock cube dissolved in a mug of boiling water. Simmer gently, stirring regularly, for half an hour, and watch how all the bite (mustard), sharpness (that acidic ketchup kick), sweetness (tomato) and different spices condense, combine and turn into something truly beautiful. These are all the weird dissonant raw ingredients of you, and just look at the dish they make: all those harsh edges melt away when these parts of the whole come together and just *be*. Season with salt and pepper and serve over mashed potatoes or rice, and reflect on how amazing it is to be a weird, flawed human recipe. Serves four.

Toffee apple rock cakes

If you can love these misshapen, lumpy, bumpy little rocks, you can sure as hell love your own wonderful body. Preheat the oven to 180°C/fan 160°C/gas mark 4. Cover 200g of dates with boiling water and leave to soften for 10–15 minutes, before draining and mashing them. Add to a large bowl along with two small peeled and grated apples, one peeled and cubed apple, 50g of raisins, 60g of soft light brown sugar, 100ml of vegetable oil, three tablespoons of milk and a teaspoon of vanilla extract. In a separate bowl, combine 250g of plain flour, two teaspoons of baking powder, three-quarters of a teaspoon of cinnamon and a good pinch of salt. Stir this dry mix into the wet ingredients until only just combined. Don't overmix, or the cakes will be heavy! Dollop into twelve mounds on a lined baking tray and cook in the oven for 25 minutes or so, until risen and springy.

Life-changing energising drink to LIFT your spirits and KICKSTART your day!

Put a can of Fanta, or Coke, or ginger beer (amen) in the fridge until it's really chilled – it should be cold enough that when you take it from the fridge, perfect little jewels of condensation cluster around the edge. Hold your breath while you crack the top, and hear the fizz, then let the hiss of gas sting your nose as you take the magic first sip. I was lying when I said it was life-changing, by the way. It's just a can of pop. But it'll feel amazing while you drink it, and isn't that enough?

Biting back

All this goes to show how important food is to us – not just as nutrition, but symbolically, as a way of representing who – and what – we are. So we should also think about what it means when we withdraw food from people – whether it's the silly, indulgent treats that make life worth living, or the basic nutrition we need to keep healthy. If our attitudes to food in general are so messed up that we muddle vegetables with salvation, and emptiness with virtue, what does that mean for the ways we treat the less fortunate among us? Because we see food as a way of coding goodness and evil, we're quick to take from the bellies of those we don't think are deserving, and grow plump on our own self-righteousness. Denial is the dish of the day, and if people don't practise it for themselves, we'll happily foist it upon them. All of this rhetoric of good and bad, excess and self-control, comes together in the four walls of the prison cell.

Food behind bars is a provocative topic. There are those who think that prisoners should be fed bread and water, and that nowadays – in this 'nanny state' age – time inside is an unfettered luxury: make wrong-doers suffer, deter others from doing wrong. Because there's such an incredible chasm between the food we fundamentally need (water, sustenance, just enough calories to keep us ticking over) and the food we enjoy (bowls of noodles in savoury broth, chicken nuggets, chunks of mature Cheddar), food is particularly fertile territory for the act of taking away. The state can fulfil its obligation to keep the prison population alive without ever making that life pleasurable.

In a study from 2016, women incarcerated in Canada's prisons at the time described prison fare as 'the worst food I've ever tasted', recalling 'mystery meat', 'green eggs' and even a pubic hair in a meal. Meanwhile, a prisoner called Sophie has become inspiration for the Food Behind Bars campaign. The movement aims to improve the food served in British prisons, where Sophie was fed such poor-quality meals that the women had to take laxatives just to be able to poo. A 2016 paper found that the budget for food per person in UK prisons was approximately £2 per day.

Because the food we eat so powerfully embodies who we are and where we stand in society, prison food not only deprives but also defines: 'slop' for nobodies, 'a dog's dinner' for animals, 'muck' for people whose humanity was long ago given up on. As prison and justice scholar Thomas Ugelvik wrote, 'Food works as a metaphor for the control over the prisoner's body', and so the system works to control that food as closely as possible. Meals are planned in advance (taking the joy of food planning from the hands of prisoners, and impinging on their ability to follow their appetite – something which most of us do without even thinking), eating conditions are cramped and often unhygienic (prisoners report eating their meals next to, or even on, their cell toilets), and food is of questionable quality and nutritional value. Each of these deprivations adds up to an assault on the mental and physical health of the people who the state is supposed to protect.

But wherever there is control, there is subversion. Turning away from the seriousness of prison to Roald Dahl for a moment: when *Matilda*'s Bruce Bogtrotter eats the entire chocolate cake that the cruel Miss Trunchbull puts in front of him, he takes what was supposed to be a punishment and spins it into a woozy, bloated, sickly act of rebellion. In the film adaptation of the book, the seeds for an uprising were sown the moment that Matilda stole two perfect, forbidden chocolates – one for her, and one for her protector, Miss Honey – from Miss Trunchbull's greedily guarded stash. Along more dystopian lines and back to the themes of control and imprisonment, in Margaret Atwood's *The Handmaid's*

Tale food is an aspect of life where enslaved Offred can claw back tiny morsels of power. She steals sugar sachets, she saves the butter from her meal and uses it to moisturise her skin. These tiny treacherous acts are glimmers of something new, different and dangerous among the tedium.

It's what's happening in some more progressive prisons, where residents are allowed to cook their own meals and even grow their own produce (though often still only as a 'perk' for good behaviour). It's what the women in the Canadian study did, in response to their 'disgusting' food, by trading meals, helping each other get the foods they needed to feel well, and trying to nourish one another when the system wouldn't. Food is much more than just fuel, and when these women resist control, they unleash the full power of food: as currency, comfort, belonging, support, community, confidence and love. These little things, far beyond the scope of what prisoners are deemed to 'deserve', are the things that make life happen.

> I can't remember what it was – but I was trying not to make any noise but I guess somebody heard me cry, and suddenly, woops, I had three girls on my bed and um one with a juice and one with a doughnut, and ok … they were talking to me and stroking my hair and hugs and ya' know? Everything that makes you feel better.

Ultimately, it'll take a revolution in the way we look at food for us to change the system. Once we can learn to see food – and not just any old food, but good, delicious, nourishing food – as a fundamental right, then we will be able to overhaul the ways that we feed the prison population, poor children, and people in care, in detention centres or hospitals. When this happens, prisoners will receive a slice of birthday cake on their big day, and schoolchildren will all sit down together and – regardless of social class or background – eat a shared meal. Hospital food will become rich and nutritious, and every patient, whether toothless, coeliac or on a Halal diet, will sit up in their bed when they hear the rattle of the dinner trolley. There will be something for everyone. When we dismantle the system that makes food and pleasure contingent upon worth, we find that we *all* deserve to eat well. No more fluffy promises of salvation from the wellness camp, no more puritanism from diet industry shills, no more food snobbery or culinary borders. The better we feed others, the better we feed ourselves. This is the key to wellness.

Emotional eating

Heart food

Adèle throws herself onto her bed, pulls a box out from underneath and grabs at the stash. She unwraps a chocolate bar and pushes it into her mouth faster than she can eat it, her face wet with tears. In this scene, in 2013 film *Blue Is the Warmest Colour*, queer heroine Adèle has just broken up with a boyfriend, and with a hunger that will resurface again throughout the film, she voraciously eats the feelings that plague her. This is emotional, impulsive self-soothing, not to mention a (slightly clunky) metaphor for all the queer appetites beginning to stir inside of her.

The pangs of hunger we feel in our bellies become muddled with countless other kinds of want: a lack of food can feel like a lack of love; a lack of love can feel like a lack of food. We turn to food, so often, to try to sate the emotional hungers that we feel, filling our stomachs with hot cross buns, chocolate milkshakes, pork pies, in a vain attempt to satisfy that niggling feeling, deep inside, that we need more from life. Leaving those emotional hungers calling is maybe the scariest thing we can do: to just sit and feel dissatisfied, fearful, furious or unfulfilled, and just let that emotion seize you, is a brave act. And so we look for comfort elsewhere, whether that's at the bottom of the bottle, the baggie or the biscuit tin. We eat our feelings, lest our feelings eat us.

The folk singer-songwriter Judee Sill knew a lot about

hunger. Up until her untimely death aged just thirty-one, she followed a path that swerved erratically between the teetering glory of her finest work – achingly sad songs about longing and love – and her lowest ebbs, marred by substance abuse, car crashes and crime. She was an addict and a musician, and these two parts of her identity spun as deftly around each other as the filaments of melody – Sill's voice split into four-part chorale – that ran through her songs.

Hunger is a theme that resurfaces throughout Sill's 1973 album, *Heart Food*. Even the title pulls our focus to a yearning that sits deep in the heart of each of us. There's *thirst*, and *guts*, and *spirit* that all pull in separate directions in Sill's songs, splintering our human experience into a million shards of pain and wonder. By the end of her life, Sill's own hunger had taken her away from her musical career into drug addiction, and she died of an overdose in 1975.

When Judee Sill sings about the gap between her spirit and her body, and the hunger that seeps in between, this isn't some dream of a bodiless existence. Sill doesn't want to let go of her earthly roots, or the unavoidable hunger that we feel as human beings: she feels every last pang of that hunger, and she cherishes it. The wonderful thing about allowing yourself to feel your hunger – whether that's the hunger that Sill sung about, or a more physical gurgling – *[raging] in my guts* – is that it reminds you of the distance between where you are, and where you want to be. When you say 'I am hungry,' you might think you're just talking about wanting another pack of Maltesers, but what you're really saying is that you're alive, and that you want more, and that there's no pleasing your soul until your body has been appeased. You are myth, intestine, splendour, fart, divinity and heaviness all at once.

I think there's a lot to be said for being reflective and considering your cravings but comfort eating gets a particularly bad reputation and I'm not here to write off this kind of eating as some weak-willed, emotional indulgence. In a culture where displays of emotional vulnerability are often seen as desperate and sad, we sometimes have no choice but to self-soothe rather than look outwards for help. We're conditioned from the moment we're born to equate food with comfort, and we carry this belief with us through every sucked thumb, soothing bedtime Horlicks and post-breakup feast.

Food has the power to patch up the ragged edges of our souls – the frayed tempers and unravelled dreams – and make the world seem OK again, if only for a few moments. All food is, to a degree, comfort food. When you raise a piece of garlic bread to your mouth after a long, taxing day, and you're hit with the heady scent of garlic and herbs, and a slick of butter coats your lips – that is comfort food. Even a floppy, soggy cheese and onion pasty, rescued from the tepid purgatory of a station café sandwich cabinet, can be comfort food if you eat it, as I once did, on the way home from visiting your sick grandad in hospital. Two days later, a glass of orange juice is comfort food, when you find out that your grandad has just died.

> alcohol units 5 (drowning sorrows), cigarettes 23 (fumigating sorrows), calories: 3,856 (smothering sorrows in fat-duvet).

In Helen Fielding's anti-literary classic, *Bridget Jones's Diary*, we see clearly this impulse to self-medicate with food and drink. Bridget is a relatable mess of cravings and compulsions and poorly cobbled together self-help plans: a kind of proto-Hannah Horvath (of Lena Dunham's hit show *Girls*). She is also the apotheosis of emotional eating. She holds a mirror to our need to – when the shit hits the fan – crack open an M&S two-pack of chocolate éclairs and eat our worries away.

Not all comfort food is made equal, and there are some foods that we turn to when times get hard in not in our individual ones and twos but as an entire nation. These are official Comfort Foods. There must be something written into our national psyche: if someone is under the weather or feeling bad, it follows as surely as if it were programmed into some psychological algorithm that someone will pitch in with the offer: 'Shall I make a cup of tea?' Food writer Laurie Colwin summed up this yearning in her trademark straight-talking style when she wrote, in *Home Cooking*: 'When people are tired and hungry, which in adult life is much of the time, they do not want to be confronted by an intellectually challenging meal: they want to be consoled.'

This is why we find our tastes turned to warm, familiar foods when we're in need of solace. We want things that thread effortlessly through the fabric of our lives: flavours that remind us of another time or, if they are new, at the very least run with the grain of our established tastes and preferences. A bar of Galaxy chocolate can be comfort food in a way that a box of single-origin 85% dark chocolate never could. A bowl of milky rice pudding – rippled through with a spoonful of raspberry jam – is way more likely to be ambrosia if it is, indeed, Ambrosia than if it's some slow-cooked fancy rice pudding in a tiny ramekin.

Every culture has its own roster of favourite comfort foods. In Ghana, it might be jollof rice, or slices of plantain fried until they're sweet, tender and golden brown. My partner, who is half Filipina, yearns for big pots of *adobo*, or sour, savoury *sinigang*, when she needs culinary comfort. The United States has a particularly strong culture of this: from mac'n'cheese, baked until burnished and bubbling, to the soothing silkiness of New England clam chowder. Ultimately, what constitutes comfort food in any given cuisine is about lack: in places where the climate is damp and cold, comfort food might be steaming and abundant; people who have access to all the food under the sun might look back to humbler soups, stews and peasant foods.

It says a great deal about us in Britain that, in the face of an increasingly scary world, we found comfort in shows like *The Great British Bake Off*. In *Bake Off*, contestants (myself among them) would go out nobly, self-effacingly, on the back of a sunken Charlotte Russe. We'd say thank you for the opportunity, and shake everyone's hand, and have a little cry about a crème anglaise. We'd shuffle and scurry and simper and, occasionally, make something magical. The magic lay in how the show eschewed the melodrama of American-style contests, with their set menu of competitiveness, sabotage and self-centredness. Instead, it was polite and neurotically perfectionist. It was pure British comfort food in several senses of the word.

And yet you have to wonder why, with Britain more diverse than ever, we chose a diet of sickly sweet cake and crumpets for our comfort food. When the state of the world requires us to be more political and proactive than ever, we find comfort in a programme that offers such a backwards-looking, nationalistic, 'Keep Calm and Carry On' vision of Britishness. For the seven seasons that *Bake Off* aired on the BBC, our national comfort food was all tea, cake and scones, lacy strings of bunting fluttering whimsically in the breeze. We closed our eyes to all the colour and vibrancy of the outside world and reframed British identity in shades of pastel. This was the purest kind of escapism. There's a lot of power in this kind of nostalgia, of course: it's why *Bake Off* topped the TV ratings year after year, and reinvigorated a national appetite for cake. But, just like the comfort food it features – the scones, cheerful cubist Battenburg cakes, éclairs and pies – we can only survive on this diet for so long. Sooner or later we need to look out into the world, be active, and use our hunger for a good cause.

Heartbreak stew with dumplings

I believe only a few things with real certainty in my heart. One is that Kim Kardashian and Kanye West share the truest and purest love that has ever been. Another is that the pain of any heartbreak can be softened with stew. Kim and Kanye will never have to worry about the latter, I'm sure.

When the post-breakup impulse is to lie prostrate on the floor refreshing Twitter and waiting for death, a stew is the thing that will keep you going. It will cloud your kitchen windows with condensation and line the air with the heady scent of home cooking; it will beg you to engage with it – from smelling the sweetness of the onions as they brown, to squeezing dumplings carefully between your hands. It's a mindful kind of cooking: the best stews are the ones that cook gently, unperturbed by anxious stirring or the restless cranking up of the oven knobs. A beef stew should cook for so long that the juices begin to catch and caramelise at the edge of the pan, and until a lone floury potato thrown in has cooked to nothingness, leaving only the faintest velvety thickness in the sauce. A stew made with chunks of butternut squash and boldly flavoured with garlic, paprika and marjoram needs to simmer until the squash is tender, and the sauce smoky and rich. There's something very healing about being quiet, watchful and patient for a while, when your whole world is teetering on the brink.

There are stews that work with mashed potatoes (although it has to be a coarse mash: fluffy, earthy, speckled with flecks of black pepper, rather than creamy, butter-laden, golden swirls of mash – as much as I love that). There are other stews that are better ladled over soft-cooked polenta or piles of steaming rice. But stews served with dumplings are the most magical. Is there anything lovelier than a dumpling? It feels strange to fuss over dumplings during the turmoil of a heartbreak. I have felt this myself, caught in that moment of discord between the raging and screaming of my soul and the gentleness of carefully nestling dumplings into a pot of steaming stew. I've even spoken to the dumplings in my madness. But that moment of strange caring is enough, sometimes, to lift you up. When everything feels hopeless, it's a reminder that there are real things in your life, things that are tangible and meaningful and even delicious, and it's up to you to bring them to fruition. I feel anchored again, like I belong in my body and my body belongs in this world, when I make something with this care. The dumplings balloon from pallid little balls to fat, steaming, glorious clouds, their bottoms sodden with savoury stew. They're as hot and heavy and beautiful as little babies.

Smoky butternut squash stew
with chickpea dumplings

I wrote this recipe for my second cookbook, *Flavour*, and I've been revisiting it whenever I'm in need of culinary comfort ever since. Sweat a large chopped onion and four crushed cloves of garlic in a very large saucepan with a couple of tablespoons of vegetable oil. When soft, add three tablespoons of harissa, a heaped teaspoon of smoked paprika, a teaspoon of ground cumin and half a teaspoon of cinnamon, to form a sweet, fragrant base for the stew. Give it a stir or two. Add five thickly sliced carrots and a peeled butternut squash, cut into 2–3cm chunks. Throw in marjoram if you can find it, oregano if you can't. Stir again. Add two tins of chopped tomatoes, and two drained tins of chickpeas. Top up with enough water to cover the veg and simmer for 40 minutes. Meanwhile, mash a drained tin of chickpeas, and mix with 150g of plain flour, 75g of vegetable suet, 2½ teaspoons of baking powder and a teaspoon each of smoked paprika and cumin. Add a pinch of salt and some finely chopped parsley leaves, before stirring in 90–110ml of cold water. Roll the dumpling mix into twelve little balls, arrange on top of the simmering stew, put a lid on and simmer for a further 20 minutes, until the dumplings are fluffy and plump. Serves 4–6.

Groundnut soup with fufu

I taught myself to make this in the aftermath of my grandad's death, trying to connect with my Ghanaian heritage. Fufu flour is made of cocoyam or plantain, and you can find it in colourful boxes in Afro-Caribbean food stores. If I can find it in Sheffield – a place with six Greggs bakeries on a single stretch of road – you can find it where you are. It makes the most wonderful dumplings, heavy and comforting. These aren't like the fluffy leavened dumplings we're used to, though: they're gummier, softer and sit in tender, almost quivering, mounds in the soup bowl.

In a large saucepan with a couple of tablespoons of vegetable oil, fry a finely sliced onion, four crushed cloves of garlic, a 5–6cm piece of ginger – peeled and finely chopped – and a whole Scotch Bonnet chilli pepper, pierced a few times with a sharp knife. Stir regularly. When the onion is tender, add four heaped tablespoons of tomato purée, and stir to combine. Add 250g of peanut butter and 1.5–2 litres of chicken or vegetable stock. Simmer for 20 minutes. Meanwhile, make the fufu according to the instructions on the box (each flour and brand is slightly different, but in essence you will be beating the flour, a little salt and water over the heat until very thick and starchy). Once the soup is ready, remove the Scotch Bonnet, squeezing it a little on its way out if you want more spice in the soup. Blend the soup in a food processor or with a stick blender until silky, then serve in shallow bowls, using a tablespoon to scoop a hefty quenelle of fufu dumpling into the middle of each bowl. Serves 4.

Old-fashioned beef stew

In our bleakest moments we need a taste of home, and here in the UK, more often than not, that means something rich, stodgy, savoury, and glorious in fifty shades of brown. You have to fry the beef first, to get that mellow richness through the sauce: make sure the pan is very hot and well oiled, then fry 750g of stewing steak for just a few minutes, cooking it in batches to avoid crowding and steaming. Set the meat aside while you sweat two roughly chopped onions with a couple of chopped carrots, a bay leaf and the leaves picked from a bunch of thyme. After 5–10 minutes over a low heat, add the beef, a mug of dark ale, two peeled and chopped potatoes, and plenty of beef stock (0.75–1 litre) to cover. Leave to simmer for a couple of hours over a low heat, the pan covered by a lid. Top up with a little boiling water as necessary.

Meanwhile, make the dumplings. Mix 200g of plain flour, 3½ teaspoons of baking powder, 100g of suet, ½ teaspoon of salt, and just enough water to make a sticky dough. Divide into 10–12 round balls. After a couple of hours, add the dumplings to the stew and put *The Way We Were* in the DVD player. The dumplings will be puffed and springy after 20 minutes or so, and by this point Barbra Streisand will be letting Robert Redford lovingly tie her shoelaces. By the time you're done with the stew and dumplings, and are halfway through a tub of ice cream, they will have broken up, and difficult, wilful, beautiful Barbra will be setting out alone. Serves six.

Sex, drugs and dopamine

Dopamine is a neurotransmitter, and it does a lot of different jobs in our brains, from enabling pleasure-like sensations associated with 'rewards', to controlling attention and regulating certain neural pathways. It's the thing that floods our brains when we do something that feels good, whether that's taking drugs or having a cream bun. It plays into our relationships with sex (kicking in at the moment of arousal), gambling (leaving us chasing our fortune long after the pennies have run out) and recreational drugs. It figures in some of the most delightful and disastrous things that we can do as humans.

But dopamine is complex, and it isn't just one thing. At its best, it's the euphoria of falling in love, or the rush of happiness we feel as we step outside and feel the sunshine on our face, but it can also help lock us into cycles of addiction, or aggravate some of the symptoms of post-traumatic stress disorder. This has resulted in no end of alarmist headlines and reductive op eds. Dopamine is a terrible, awful, chemical thing, some papers tell us, while throwing around the threat of crack cocaine, addiction and death like beach balls on a blithe summer day. Fear its siren call! It is also, so we're told, a blissful syrupy elixir, bringing us all one step closer to mindful, meditative godliness, all toned bodies and glass-half-full minds. If only we could have more!

Cookbooks, celebrities and diet faddists play into this second fallacy with exuberant abandon – the main example being from TV chef Tom Kerridge. His cookbook, *Tom Kerridge's Dopamine Diet*, champions high-protein 'dopamine-enhancing' foods, such as fresh fish, meat and eggs, and encourages us to do away with carbohydrates. What's the harm in this, you might ask. Kerridge, looking like a slimmed-down, somewhat frantic version of his former self, informs us that certain foods facilitate dopamine production in the brain because they contain a compound called tyrosine. If we can up our consumption of this wonder drug, we'll be slimmer, more content, and more able to scrape our lazy carcasses out of bed and throw ourselves headlong into the world! It's a miracle.

Except, it's not. There's no condensing happiness – or the complicated neurochemistry behind dopamine – down to a simple question of good and bad foods. In early 2017, the British Dietetic Association (BDA), an official body for UK-based dietitians, released a report looking at some of the more spectacular claims of the year's crop of diet books. In this report, the BDA noted: '[Tom Kerridge's] specific claim that high-protein foods bring joy is a massive over-promise based on very theoretical concepts. There are no human studies showing that more proteins in the diet translate to more dopamine levels in brain tissue.'

In fact, *Tom Kerridge's Dopamine Diet* is nothing new at all. This low-carbohydrate, high-protein diet just rides the bandwagon that started its trundling progress with the Atkins diet and which now, pushing forward with the momentum of a runaway train, underpins everything from fashionable gluten-free regimes to the paleo diet. Kerridge sets the scene for us to emerge from weight loss like a glorious phoenix from the embers of our slothful former selves, but for all the talk of dopamine and happiness and some fantastical emotional rebirth, this cookbook – and others like it – are little more than souped-up versions of the weight-loss movements that came before.

As the BDA recognises, there is no formula for dopamine-induced bliss, far less a recipe for a high-protein, low-carb dopamine-induced bliss. We need *all* food groups – carbohydrates, proteins and fats, as well as a host of vitamins and minerals – in order to give ourselves the building blocks of happiness. It's true that foods such as egg and fish contain compounds that can help us, in theory, create dopamine. But it's also the case that *all* food, to varying degrees, sets off dopamine-releasing alarms in our brains. And contrary to the dictates of the dopamine diet, carbs are actually pretty useful when it comes to fuelling happiness. Carbohydrates can affect the levels of certain amino acids in our bloodstream, and when they do this, they free up space for something called tryptophan to be taken into the brain. Tryptophan then enables the production of serotonin, a neurotransmitter which is linked to feelings of contentedness.

Tom Kerridge isn't alone in delivering such big, problematic promises. We're currently right in the middle of a tidal wave of food-based medicine: healthy-eating books with words like 'doctor', 'medicine', 'cure' and 'healing' in the titles. I even found one questionable diet book on Amazon called *Food Is Better Medicine Than Drugs: Don't Go to Your Doctor Before Reading This Book*. What this movement has created is a sense not only that certain foods (gluten, processed meats, and so on) can ultimately kill you, but that other foods can save you. It's little surprise that the people behind these kinds of books slip into expressing other kinds of 'holistic' health care and well-being claims. Gwyneth Paltrow's infamous lifestyle website Goop recommends putting jade eggs up your vagina in the name of 'detoxing'. Alkaline diet hawker Natasha Corrett has expressed nervousness on her blog about the side effects of common vaccines. This culture snowballs into a distrust of doctors, and a belief that if you eat, drink, exercise, live just so, you can ward off disease. The subtext is, of course, that if you try hard enough, you can stave off death.

But there's no guarantee that our diet will lead us straight to happy-ever-after. The underlying assumption of these diets – that we can figure out the ingredients for happiness, and eat our way to success – is a dangerous idea. Our bodies and brains are so much more endlessly complex than we could ever imagine. No matter what we do, there's no way to guarantee health. Without a doubt, a diet of Coca-Cola and cornflakes isn't going to lead you to your best self. But nor will a sanitised diet of leafy greens with a side of self-righteousness. You cannot write a recipe for happiness. Happiness, and sadness, and everything in between, are impossible to predict. This is the neurological equivalent of Carrie Bradshaw's famous 'I couldn't help but wonder ...' It's the magic of just rolling with the weird twists and turns, metaphors and segues along the path, and not trying to cheat fate by getting to happiness as the crow flies.

The worry trap

It's not just diets promising untold (and unscientific) benefits that can destabilise the way we think about food. Scare stories – about gluten, mysterious 'toxins', dairy – abound, and can drench us in unnecessary guilt and anxiety. Let's talk about MSG. Monosodium glutamate is a flavour enhancer, doing much the same job as salt. You can buy it online and in plenty of East Asian food stores cheaply enough, and it's commonly used in certain areas of Japanese and Chinese cooking. It is simple stuff: salt, and glutamate (a compound found naturally in cheese, tomatoes and much more). MSG even has a cute origin story: a Japanese professor, Kikunae Ikeda, took a sip of his wife's soup and remarked that it tasted even better than usual. The secret was, it turned out, in the *kombu* – a variety of edible kelp – used to form the soup's *dashi* broth. From that sip of soup, Ikeda went on to unmask all of the secrets of that savoury, moreish flavour, carefully homing in on the glutamate contained in the *kombu*. Ikeda had taken a bite from the fruit of the tree of knowledge, and all the marvels of taste lay there for him to grow rich on. He stabilised the glutamate he extracted by adding salt, and monosodium glutamate was born.

It wasn't long before MSG found its way across the oceans to America and Europe. It became popular in factory-made foods including tinned foods, although take-up by the home cook was slower. In 1959, an article about MSG in the *Observer* about the wonder of the chemical bemoaned that 'as yet there is no British firm that packets M.S.G. to sell it retail, so it is worth suggesting to your grocer that he buys it loose from the wholesaler and sells it to you in small quantities'. There is, the writer – bylined only as Syllabub – reassures us, 'a good margin of profit'. The article wraps, delightfully, with a recipe for 'Halibut Casserole with M.S.G.'.

And then came the fall from grace. In 1968, a letter to the *New England Journal of Medicine* described something dubbed 'Chinese restaurant syndrome'. The letter described a sense of general malaise and weakness after eating out at American Chinese restaurants. It set off a chain reaction that Alan Levinovitz describes in his book, *The Gluten Lie*: 'Less than two months after [the letter was published], *The New York Times* ran an article under the headline "Chinese Restaurant Syndrome Puzzles Doctors". Within six months, the prestigious journal *Nature* published research by scientists who definitively identified MSG as the culprit – and, alarmingly, pointed out that it lurked everywhere, not just in Chinese food: TV dinners, canned goods, seasoning, even baby food.'

As quickly as it had come, MSG fell out of favour, and it carries its bad reputation with it to this very day. *Everyone* seemed to have a story about how awful they'd felt after Chinese food. Everyone had some undiagnosable ailment with fuzzy edges that looked, if you squinted, like a reaction to some poison. This was a public health disaster drummed up through the steady rhythm of scaremongering newspaper

headlines, fear of the unknown and, as usual, a seasoning
of racism. A fearful Western public enthusiastically turned
against this unfamiliar, suspiciously foreign-sounding thing
and, with its three cold little letters and its clinical, untrust-
worthy chemical name, MSG was thrown unceremoniously
out with the garbage.

And yet this awful chemical, this poison, shipped straight
from foreign shores to an unsuspecting American public
turned out to be completely harmless. Again, and again, and
again, the health risks of MSG have been debunked. None
of those symptoms – from 'head fog' to palpitations – were
attributable to monosodium glutamate when trials were conducted scientifically, rigorously, away from the media storm.
The whole furore had been for nothing.

This isn't to say that people's symptoms were fake. There's
something relevant here in the fact that most of us in the UK
and the United States rarely eat Chinese food, and when we
do, we *really* eat it. Giddy on the thrill of the Big Night In, we
feast on a tray of sweet and sour, half a dozen spring rolls,
far too much of a Peking duck, and a bottle of wine, before
wondering where it all went wrong. The most powerful driver
in the panic pandemic, though, isn't necessarily what we do,
or don't, put in our stomachs. The ingredients for illness are
all right here already, right between our ears. Quite often, it's
all in our heads.

Galen, a Greek physician and early medical scholar,
reported nearly 2,000 years ago:

I was called in to see a woman, who was stated to be sleepless at night and to lie tossing about from one position
into another. Finding she had no fever, I made a detailed
inquiry into everything that had happened to her, especially considering such factors as we know to cause
insomnia. But she either answered little or nothing at all,

as if to show that it was useless to question her. Finally, she turned away, hiding herself completely by throwing the bedclothes over her whole body, and laying her head on another small pillow, as if desiring sleep.

After leaving I came to the conclusion that she was suffering from one of two things; either from a melancholia dependent on black bile, or else trouble about something she was unwilling to confess.

By much of contemporary medical thinking, an imbalance of melancholic black bile would have been the end of the story. A physical symptom (in this case, insomnia) must have a physical cause. But, in a kind of gossipy sleuthing that *Legally Blonde*'s Elle Woods herself would be proud of, Galen stepped out of the shadow of his forebears, and made an intellectual leap:

When somebody came from the theatre and said that he had seen Pylades dancing, both her expression and the colour of her face changed. Seeing this, I applied my hand to her wrist and noticed that her pulse suddenly became extremely irregular. This kind of pulse indicates that the mind is disturbed thus it occurs also in people who are disputing over any subject … Thus I found out that the woman was in love with Pylades, and by careful watch on the succeeding days my discovery was confirmed.

The woman's physical symptoms were, Galen surmised, the result not of the humours – heavy, physical things – but of fluttering, awful love. It might all look very obvious to the modern mind, but this was a massive cognitive leap. If that one patient's pulse could play hopscotch at just the thought of handsome Pylades, then there might be other physical symptoms that could be traced back to the brain. If the brain had the potential to send our body reeling, then perhaps the power to stop illness lay with us, too. Maybe, we eventually began to suspect, it's all in our heads. In the case of MSG, it was.

There's a lot to be said for this idea in an age of mass paranoia about food and eating. More and more people are coming forward with self-diagnosed allergies, ailments and intolerances. The market for gluten-free foods has boomed, despite the fact that only 1% of the population is estimated to suffer from coeliac disease, and a mere 5% can lay claim to a less severe kind of gluten sensitivity. The market for lactose-free milks has grown, and the consumption of non-peanut nut butters has exploded. This is an industry so big that, at any given point in the last year or so, roughly 70% of the best-selling Food & Drink books on Amazon were about health, diet and weight loss.

The diet industry is huge and incredibly powerful, with some real despots holding the reins at the top (I'm looking at you, fake doctors, and you, fad weight-loss gurus). For every sales spike in this cynical business, there are thousands upon thousands of individual people – each one of them as worried and human as the rest of us – unintentionally stoking these fires. These people aren't silly or self-serving, they are scared. They are worried about their place in this increasingly troubled and fragile world. They are nervous that our health care system won't be there in future, and that they'll have to take health into their own hands. They are you and I and everyone we know. They are my girlfriend, for a start.

My girlfriend thought she had a lactose intolerance. There was a history of it in the family, and she didn't like how milk made her feel – bloated and panicked and inauspiciously gurgling – and so she steered clear of dairy. We got soya ice cream and almond milk, and kept cheese to a minimum. If we had a milkshake or a milky hot drink, her stomach would seize. But then we went to Italy. We had the most delicious cappuccino, and a pastry with sweet cream inside. We had gelato once … or twice … an hour … all summer. We had snowy mounds of Parmesan on plates piled high with pasta. And not once in all this time did Leah's belly so much as murmur. When we got back to England, and to all the dreariness of our flat and the unromantic reality of a shitty Kenco made with nearly-off milk, suddenly the lactose problems returned. Funny enough, though, the burping and all the other nasty symptoms that I daren't mention, never cropped up when we ate tubs of caramel-streaked dairy ice cream, or doused midsummer strawberries in cream.

After a lifetime of somewhat patchy lactose intolerance, Leah realised that it wasn't intolerance that wrung her stomach through a mangle at the sight of a glass of milk. It wasn't lactose or dairy or industrial milk pasteurisation methods. It was milk, plain and simple. She hates liquid milk. That's it. And that fear of the white stuff wreaks havoc on her ability to stomach it, or anything like it. When she is having an awful day, her defences down and anxiety up, yoghurt, cream cheese and milkshake are all off limits, guilty by association. The symptoms she feels on those days are as real as the ground we walk on. Sickness is still sickness when it's in our minds, and it's perfectly possible to suffer a nocebo effect (like a placebo effect, except you feel worse – not better – thanks to the power of anxiety, stress and nervous anticipation). But when all the stars are aligned and ABBA is on the radio and she feels the caress of the sun on the nape of her neck, Leah feels bolstered and brave.

There are, of course, food intolerances and allergies. You might be allergic to nuts, or have coeliac disease. Perhaps a lactose intolerance means you can't have dairy. If you do, of course it's really important to eat safely, and healthily, and to heed the advice of your doctor. But for those of us who haven't been diagnosed with an allergy or intolerance, it's worth thinking back to Galen and that lovesick patient sometimes. We live in a really scary world, and it seems to get progressively more terrible and dystopian every damn day that we wake up and turn on the news. The future of everything – including the NHS, our climate, and basic financial support – is looking bleaker than ever. It's no wonder we're scared. It's not surprising that we hold tighter and tighter to the few things that we still have control of: namely, our bodies, and the food we put into them.

When we hear, then, that gluten is 'glue' for the gut, it's normal and natural to be scared. The effects of anxiety and stress on our digestive systems are well known. It's understandable to start feeling a bit nervous around pasta and big carb-heavy feasts. It makes perfect sense that this anxiety would rain down through your body, settling in the pit of your stomach, and puffing your belly out in gassy, painful protest. Before long, perhaps the very thought of a bread roll leaves your belly groaning. You cut wheat out. You avoid most cakes and even the eternal glory of a Greggs sausage roll. You learn to be on high alert, checking ingredient lists and labels at every turn. This anxiety has found a permanent home in your body, and it positively insists on your food intolerance at every turn. If you didn't have a bodily reaction to gluten to start with, you sure will now.

Nutritionist Michelle Allison, who I'll introduce properly in the following section (Bittersweet, page 103), wrote about this anxiety, and the awfulness of choice, in an article for *The Atlantic*. 'Overwhelmed by choice, by the dim threat of mortality that lurks beneath any wrong choice, people crave rules from outside themselves, and successful heroes to guide them to safety.' We are all scared, and want nothing more than to be swaddled tight in the grasp of a diet industry that tells us that a pea-protein shake is the one true way to save your soul.

Bittersweet

There are times when the labours of your mind and the contents of your stomach work together in symphony. A good mood leads you to a glass of ice-cold lemonade; chips glistening with salt spike the pleasure chemicals in your brain. At that moment, your body and mind exist in a kind of harmony: eating is wholesome and uncomplicated, and nourishes every cell of you. And in this nourishment, you are a whole person, mind and body, body and mind, not knotted or conflicted or anxious. For a second, you just *exist*.

Most of the time, though, food is more complicated than that. We are human, and we have sharp edges, aches and pains, heavy burdens to carry. We don't just drift through the world like some kind of beneficent peace-and-love plasma – life snags on us like thorns. Because food exists at the interface between us and everything else, eating can be particularly troublesome when we're not at peace with the world around us. When we don't know exactly what we want from life, food can be difficult. When our bodies feel too big or small, eating can be awful.

For some of us, these moments of unease take root, furrowing deep into the very essence of our relationship with food. This is what it is to have an eating disorder. People with anorexia, bulimia, binge-eating disorder and certain forms of body dysmorphia live in regular or constant anxiety, their body sitting uncomfortably in the world, and their mind at loggerheads with the needs of that body. The ways that these eating disorders operate are very different from person to person: for some, it might mean eating too much, for others too little. It could be exercising to excess, or losing control when eating.

I had an eating disorder for several years: a disorientating ride between undereating, overeating and purging, sometimes coming full circle several times within the course of a single day. I was never officially diagnosed, despite having come into contact with health care professionals who recognised the problem, but I was deeply unwell. Technically, I suppose, my symptoms were akin to bulimia, with some binge eating and anorexia on the side. But labels aren't necessarily important for everyone. Descend too deep into the vocabulary of diagnoses, and we risk alienating those whose symptoms straddle different conditions. If we concentrate too hard on formalised criteria for eating disorders, we can leave out those who don't consider themselves to be unhappy or thin enough to be 'truly' ill. Anorexia, bulimia, binge-eating disorder and other uncategorised eating disorders will manifest in very different ways in different sufferers, and there are as many ways to be ill as there are people. In fact, the very term – 'eating disorder' – suggests a pathology that can send people scurrying for the exit. What is important is that at the heart of all kinds of disordered eating is an acute anxiety around food.

The reasons for this anxiety are different for everyone. Perhaps you've grown to lean too heavily on the calming, saccharine relief of biting a Mars Bar. Maybe some trauma has left you wanting to unburden yourself of this heavy, painful body you carry around: not eating is a pretty direct way to spite your physical self. It could just be that years and years of socially endorsed (or even enforced) dieting, calorie counting and 'New Year, New You' promises have worn away at your bodily barometers, and you no longer know what hunger feels like. Maybe there is no stand-out reason, maybe you're just anxious and sad and confused about food, and you don't know why. This is OK, too.

What we know is that eating disorders affect over 1.6 million people in the UK, but that this estimate traces a tentative lower limit. Because mental health conditions exist so often in secret, and because mental health care resources are stretched so thinly, the true scope of eating disorders is thought to be significantly higher. We also know that the majority of these sufferers are women. And in case you're hung up on the idea that eating disorders are all about weight, there's actually a lot of data showing that those with eating disorders overlap substantially with those who self-harm – this is about self-esteem, anxiety, pain and control. There's an idea that nutritionist and dietitian Michelle Allison talks about on her website, The Fat Nutritionist: *permission* – giving yourself permission to eat what feels right, when it feels good, and in the amounts that you choose. When our eating becomes disordered, this permission becomes a curse, a burden of choice too great to shoulder.

The cruelty of eating disorders is that they strip us of one of the few certainties we have in a deeply intangible, difficult world: that our bodies know what we need, and that our appetite will guide us there. Eating disorders muddle the signals of our supposedly self-regulating human bodies, until we scarcely know what we want, when or how. In this context, the idea of comfort eating becomes thorny. What might be a necessary, soul-nurturing indulgence for someone with a good relationship with food, might be a slippery slope for someone with an eating disorder.

When I sing the praises of comfort eating, then, it bears saying that there are some urges and impulses that we should pause and consider before we indulge them. If eating what you want means eating nothing, that's disordered eating. If eating what you want means bingeing, barely tasting the food in front of you, eating until you feel ill, and long past the point of comfort, that's disordered eating. Done in isolation these things are not particularly bad, but we ought to be mindful of how these behaviours fit together, and what the bigger picture looks like for us and the food we eat. If this kind of food-related anxiety makes a regular appearance in your life, take hold of it – look that anxiety in the eye, acknowledge it, and ask for help in whatever way you can, whether that's from friends, family or a therapist.

And yet, it's OK to slip up. One wrongfooted foray into a Wagon Wheel multipack doesn't mean that the world is ending! A day when your stomach is so knotted with nerves that you can barely eat doesn't mean you're slipping into illness. Registered dietitian Ellyn Satter has a quote which I love so much that I can almost repeat it by heart:

> Normal eating is going to the table hungry and eating until you are satisfied. It is being able to choose food you like and eat it and truly get enough of it – not just stop eating because you think you should. Normal eating is being able to give some thought to your food selection so you get nutritious food, but not being so wary and restrictive that you miss out on enjoyable food. Normal eating is giving yourself permission to eat sometimes because you are happy, sad or bored, or just because it feels good. Normal eating is mostly three meals a day, or four or five, or it can be choosing to munch along the way. It is leaving some cookies on the plate because you know you can have some again tomorrow, or it is eating more now because they taste so wonderful. Normal eating is overeating at times, feeling stuffed and uncomfortable. And it can be undereating at times and wishing you had more. Normal eating is trusting your body to make up for your mistakes in eating. Normal eating takes up some of your time and attention, but keeps its place as only one important area of your life.

We all have moments when we let our appetites carry us places that we perhaps shouldn't go, and that's normal and fine. Eating well means eating with compassion for yourself – for the bad and the good inside of you, and for all of the lumps, bumps, beauty and ugliness on the outside. That's tough for everyone from time to time, but even more so if you have an eating disorder. There's one thing I always try to remember, though, when I can feel the tendrils of my old eating disorder creeping back into my mind: treat yourself how you'd treat your best friend. If you would be patient and forgiving with your best friend during a mental health hiccup, then you deserve that, too. If you'd make your friend a fortifying soup, give yourself that kindness. Look after yourself like a fragile, precious thing.

Relish

I have a body, and it exists in a fragile world, and I choose to relish it. I relish walking past a Portuguese bakery once, twice, three times before I muster the courage to go in and order a perfect custard tart, like a tiny, golden sun. I relish the aching feeling before a big meal with an empty stomach, and the wonder of a crumpet plucked straight from the glaring teeth of the toaster. I have decided that I will relish swiping the edge of the honey jar, decorated with sticky rivulets, with a greedy finger. My friend Soleil Ho, who co-hosts a food podcast called *Racist Sandwich*, once said to me that she likes to explode the minds of children by telling them that when you are a grown-up, you can eat ice cream any time you want. Imagine the glory of realising, for the very first time, that one day you will be able to taste the coolest, sweetest joy whenever you please. That is something to relish. When eating becomes difficult, mired in all the awfulness and heaviness of life, shock yourself anew with the magic of this freedom. All the world's pleasure is at your fingertips, in shades of caramel, velvet pistachio, mint chocolate chip. You can have ice cream any time you want.

And looking at one single label on a jar, he felt himself gone round the calendar to that private day this summer when he had looked at the circling world and found himself at its center. The word on the jar was RELISH. And he was glad he had decided to live.

Ray Bradbury, *Dandelion Wine*

Digested: A friendship

The cake was four layers high and rippled thick with ganache. I had piped 'Happy Birthday!' on top in quivering ribbons of white chocolate, but the words were too stark against the dark shimmer of the icing, and I found myself filling in the gaps with stupid stars and squiggles and swirls to crowd out the sentiment. By the time it was done, I fucking hated it, but I'd spent half the day making it, and all I'd ever seen Catherine cook was lentils, so I figured I'd won already. I carried it through to the front room, bracing my elbows against my hips just to support the weight of the thing. I must be the only person who can turn walking into a room full of tipsy people with a two-kilo chocolate cake into an anti-climax, but that's exactly what I did: sidled in, looked at the floor, deposited the cake next to Catherine like a cat dropping a limp rat on the doorstep, tapped her on the shoulder, watched her cringe with the overstatement of it all, and slipped back into the kitchen. I don't know if she even ate it, but it's just as well because I'm pretty sure it was dry anyway.

Before we shared that flat together, I barely knew Catherine. We'd only had a couple of tutorials together. When we went into the rabbit warren philosophy department, the last dregs of the afternoon would still be spilling across the Thames. By the time we came out, our brains numbed with Kant or Nozick or whatever other very clever dull man we'd imbibed, it was pitch black, and the air was wet and thick. I'd sometimes see

Catherine then, inching her way along the Strand, high heels clipping the pavement, mac tied tight around her waist. It never occurred to me that I'd ever know this person who was small and feminine and clever, with a pinched little nose and darting eyes. I was tall and gruff with alien features and a stare fixed on my feet. I would eat a corner shop samosa in stolen mouthfuls on the bus home, lining my coat pocket with crumbs.

Somehow, though, I ended up living with Catherine. We found the flat in Finsbury Park that we'd share with two mutual friends, and on the day that Catherine and I signed the lease, we went out for lunch together. We got to know each other over a huge platter of injera bread, stewed spinach and fragrant Ethiopian stews. The dish was set between us, and everything was there to be shared. I started off bold, ripping at the bread and grabbing at stew, before quickly backing off as the territory grew contested. Whose mouthful was that, and who did that part of the flatbread belong to, and what claim did my greedy fingers have to this or that nugget of goodness. I inched around the plate and waited for a stalemate to congeal around the final unclaimed morsels in the centre. But Catherine carried on eating. She ate the squash and tomato and greens and bread with her own momentum, sweeping right over some foods, wiping the dish clean of others. She didn't pause to ask me begrudgingly if I wanted the last mouthful, she didn't eat a single thing she didn't want to, or hold back from a single thing she did. I – anxious, self-effacing, disingenuous, still hungry – felt my sensibilities sticking in my throat, and I guess in a way I fell in love.

We clashed a lot. I made big pots of food for everyone whether they wanted it or not; Catherine slunk into the kitchen to cook alone, and eat alone. I was proud and ostentatious with my cooking, and commandeered the kitchen with baking pans, heavy loaves and cherry pies; she would carve the dinners from a single head of cabbage for a whole week. Despite coming *from similar working-class backgrounds and finding similarly incongruous paths into the privileged world of undergrad philosophy students, we quickly fell apart. I spent all my time testing recipes and buying new clothes and surrounding myself with sweet treats like Sofia Coppola's* Marie Antoinette *(a film that Catherine hated, by the way). On opposite sides of the kitchen, we'd dance out of one another's way, each tracking the other's silent path through our peripheral vision. I would shove some lovingly seasoned dinner or lunch box or cake (that birthday cake) in her direction, because I thought she was brilliant and effervescent and I wanted her to know that, without me having to say a single word. She would dish me up a little of her food and, over dinner, spike me with insults so tiny I could never quite be sure what had bitten me. I threw her dishes into a heap on the side before she'd had a chance to even finish chewing. She eyed me suspiciously over her aubergine.*

Food was the vocabulary that Catherine and I shared in our difficult friendship. It was often sour, sometimes rancid, regularly pilfered or uninvitedly proffered. We spoke, made up, feuded and bonded through mouthfuls of feta, porridge, rice, éclairs, chorizo, halloumi, doughnuts, mushroom, cabbage and egg. The more troubled we were, the more food I thrust upon her; the more aggressively I gave, the less she would share. And yet, every now and again, we'd meet in the middle of a food-laden table, knives down, and we would talk about all the people we hated and everything would turn to glitter. In her company, I was hungry for every scrap of knowledge and wit that she had. This is how it curdles when you have a relationship that's both sparkling and doomed. To cook is to give, to eat together is to combine the fabric of yourself with someone else. We worm our way into the hearts of the people we love, and we get there through their stomachs.

Sharing plates

On living and dying in a time of waffles

We live in a time of waffles.

I feel dizzy when I start thinking about chance, because the chances of anything happening, or having happened, seem so tiny. This book might never have happened – I could have taken a different fork in the road at any one of the million infinitesimally small, trivial decisions I've made in my life. I could have missed a crucial phone call, or met a different group of friends, been late for a train. I could never have existed at all. You could never have existed either. But when the odds are stacked against you, it makes the tiny little coincidences even more remarkable. It is a miracle that you are here, and that you are here now in this most auspicious moment in history. Because in the 200,000 years that modern humans have walked this earth, waffles have only existed for a few minuscule, sparkling moments in all of history. Waffle irons that were used to make unleavened *oublies* – an ancestor of the waffle, and a little like a communion wafer – have existed since the ninth century, but leavened waffles, as we would recognise them today, have only been around since roughly the sixteenth century. That's less than a quarter of a per cent of the span of human history. The flash of life that is you, your life – it coincides with the age of books and waffles. What a time to be alive.

There's nothing special about waffles when you flatten

them to a few words on a sheet of paper: they're just a simple batter, usually wheat flour, water or milk, egg and some kind of raising agent, such as baking powder or yeast, cooked between two irons. But waffles don't exist on the page, they exist on the plate, and it's here that they take on a life of their own. There are heavy, caramel-lined *stroopwafels* in the Netherlands, set over a steaming mug of coffee until the toffee is sticky and warm, or thick, sugar-lump-studded Belgian waffles, little toaster waffles so sweet they hurt your teeth. There are Vietnamese pandan leaf-infused waffles, rich with coconut milk, and American-style breakfast waffles heaped with scrambled eggs, maple syrup and bacon. They can be chewy and thin, bread-like and savoury, cakey, gooey or crisp.

But somehow their magic isn't even really about how they taste. Of course, they taste good (particularly – trust me on this – topped with ripe raspberries and soft mild goat's cheese whipped with double cream, drizzled with honey and finished with a liberal handful of chopped pistachios), but there's more to it than that. Why, whenever I eat breakfast out, do I linger forever on the waffle option, no matter how overblown or underdone I know it will be? The answer has very little to do with what waffles actually *are*, and everything to do with what they stand for. Nora Ephron knew this.

I Remember Nothing is full of food. It's the director and screenwriter's last published book, and in it she talks at great length about a meatloaf that was once named after her, and how the mushroom sauce with it ought not to have been served on the side, after all. There's an entire story about who should have made the dessert, and another on chicken soup. In the final essay of this final book, Nora gives us a list of things that she will miss when she dies. She will miss her husband and her children and the park, but she will also miss butter, dinner with friends, pie, ordering 'one for the table'.

She will miss not just waffles but also, in an entry all to itself, 'the concept of waffles'. Just two years after the book was published, Nora died of an illness that, it turns out, she'd known about all along, while she wrote about the things she would miss: waffles, the concept of waffles, pie.

The concept of waffles is the idea that breakfast is there to be savoured, slowly, on a Sunday morning. The concept of waffles is that you can pile indulgence on top of decadence and finish it with a drizzle of hedonism, and that this constitutes a real and valid meal. The concept of waffles is that a waffle will never, ever be a staple food, or a convenience food, or a health food, and that it is all the more special for this uselessness. They are just there to be enjoyed.

When *I Remember Nothing* was first published, it had mixed reviews. Reviewers asked one question again, and again: where is the substance? But this stuff – that they called 'fluffy' – was never just fluff. When Ephron talked about a silly row with a friend, or hating email, or waffles, she wrote the minutiae of her life big and bold. These things aren't particularly political, and they don't have the same feminist clout as Ephron's earlier essays on sexism, but these are the things that give life colour. It's important to care about handbags, going on dates, waffles, emails – all of the silly, forgettable, delicious little things that make up life and make life worth living. The bulk of our lives is scrawled in the margins. This is the stuff that matters.

Of course, it's not just waffles that we're lucky to coexist with. Think about Wotsits – at what other point in history could you have bought a crinkly packet of luminous orange cheese dust, blown up into featherweight little nuggets? Viennetta is a modern miracle! (How can ice cream be so intricately shaped, and be so soft, and taste of nothing at all?) We can eat popping candy and fake meat and foods from every corner of the earth. All of these things that are silly, and tasty, and completely unnecessary: we live in the age of these things. What a shame it would be if we didn't try our best to taste every last weird and wonderful product on the supermarket shelves, and take a moment every now and again to step away from sensibility, necessity, nutrition, and just taste something good. Look around at how lucky you are to be alive right now! But enough … I'm waffling.

Being mouthy

Food found a way into everything Nora Ephron did, including places where it really needn't have featured at all. What does a big glossy romantic comedy like *When Harry Met Sally* have to do with food? How could potatoes possibly be relevant to a story of star-crossed lovers (*Sleepless in Seattle*)? But Nora knew that when we talk about food, we're rarely just talking about food.

Take *Heartburn*, Nora's semi-autobiographical rendering of her difficult divorce. First it was a novel, and then a film, with Meryl Streep playing Rachel 'basically-Nora' Samstat, and Jack Nicholson her philandering husband. When we see Rachel make her soon-to-be husband a plate of carbonara in bed, we know that this isn't just a plate of pasta. This is the first meal that she will cook for this man who she will eventually fall in love with, then marry, and then divorce. It says 'I'm not embarrassed to care', 'I want you to see my undignified, human appetite', even 'love me, already'. And, of course, it's no coincidence that the meal Rachel cooks in that languorous, post-coital haze is a silky-smooth tangle of garlicky, rich, salty spaghetti. This is food with something to say.

Food has been a stand-in for words for as long as we have been talking and eating. It shouldn't come as a surprise that there would be a muddling between the words that come out of our mouths and the food that goes in: this is where we communicate, with our mouths, lips, tongues, teeth. Bring your lips close together, almost pursed, and hold your tongue halfway back in your mouth, push the air through your teeth. *Ffffff*. Pull your mouth into a little zero and make an *ooooooo* sound that hangs just between your lips. With your mouth slightly ajar, flick your tongue lightly against the front of the roof of your mouth as you breathe out. *Duh. F-oo-d.*

Food is a kind of language. No, really. It stands for so much more than nutrition. I often think that if I were explaining – to an alien or a big sentient plant or some other creature that had no concept of what it was to eat – what food really means to us, I'd tell them about Gemma Collins in the *Celebrity Big Brother* house. Picture the scene: Gemma, best known for being a kind-hearted, pub landlady-style loudmouth on the hit TV series *The Only Way Is Essex*, is in the garden comforting CBB housemate Tiffany, who is from the United States. Being American, and also a little prickly in her own way, Tiffany is struggling to fit in. She's said or done something silly and everyone's in a mood with her. 'Babe, tea and coffee's everythin',' Gemma says. 'It is?' 'It means a lot to people.' 'It does?' 'Yeah. It's like a heartly gesture. "Can I make you a tea?" It's like saying, "Can I give you a grand?"'

Anthropologists, scientists and social theorists have studied and hypothesised for decades about the ways that food has functioned as social currency – how it can stand in for words, act as a translator and an intermediary even between those of us who have no shared language or culture – before Gemma from TOWIE summed it all up effortlessly. When we offer someone food, we're saying we care, and certain foods carry that cultural weight more than others. A cup of tea can mean everything, especially after a long day's work, after a tiff, or when the person you love has got up five minutes early to make it, and bring it to you in bed.

You don't have to look far to find food standing in for

language. Our culture is ripe with these references. In *Moonstruck*, Cher unashamedly barges into Nicolas Cage's kitchen and cooks him a steak, insisting on feeding him whether he likes it or not. Aladdin offers two homeless children his last crust of bread. Remember *that* carbonara in *Heartburn*, or Grandpa Joe spending his last pennies buying Charlie a Wonka bar in *Charlie and the Chocolate Factory*. In the film *The Lunchbox*, a mix-up sees a housewife's tenderly made lunchboxes for her husband being sent to a perfect stranger. Being cooked for softens the stranger's prickly defences; knowing her food is being enjoyed fills the woman with pride; watching the whole thing unfold makes me weep every time.

When it comes to food and film, it's Barry Jenkins's 2016 film *Moonlight* that paints food, and feeding, the most vibrantly. Food stretches wide across the cinema screen in this coming-of-age tale of black queerness: from the young Chiron, then 'Little', eating his fill at the table of the couple who take him in; to the diner meal that Little shares with his semi-adoptive kind-of dad, Juan; to – in the final act of the film, and with the once scrawny Chiron now grown into beautiful, brusque 'Black' – the *arroz con pollo* that his ex-lover Kevin cooks for him. The food is rich and exquisite and larger than life, but it's not really the contents of the plate that count. What matters, in each of these scenes, is that the meal sits there on the table between Chiron and the people who love him – a symbol of the most nurturing kind of love. In a world that sketches the crudest caricatures of a harsh, uncaring black masculinity, the way that food stands in for an almost maternal kind of tenderness and compassion in *Moonlight* is no coincidence. This is the nourishing, emboldening reality of queer black love. Sitting down to eat that final meal, under the softly curious gaze of the man he once loved, Chiron takes out his gold grills, and takes up his fork, and eats.

Again and again, we see how food is elevated far beyond

its nutritional value. We trade these symbols – chocolates for romantic love, oysters for virility, chicken soup for motherly love – just as readily as we exchange words, and so food takes on a metaphorical life of its own. Kenyan-born philosopher John Mbiti said, in *African Religions and Philosophy*: 'I am because we are, and since we are, therefore I am.' Forget the insular, self-contained 'I' of Western philosophy: this is a very different worldview to the one Descartes proposed when he famously wrote 'I think, therefore I am.' Community is the essence of self, here, and otherness becomes a blurry, imprecise thing. If the barriers between us and those around us aren't the fixed, impermeable things we thought they were, then food is at the heart of this shared selfhood. Food transgresses the 'boundaries' between here and there, us and them, me and you, until we are all just bundles of matter, eating and being eaten. When we feed each other, we give a bit of ourselves to form the fabric of someone else. This is the glue that binds us.

I can still remember the first meal I cooked for my now-fiancée. I made pancakes for her after the first night that we spent together. I had slipped the question coyly into our getting-to-know-you chats the evening before: 'What's your favourite film? Marry-bang-kill, One Direction? *What's your favourite breakfast?*' And so I slunk out of bed first thing in the morning and ran – actually ran – to the shop to get eggs, lemons and honey. When I got back, I made a batch of really god-awful pancakes, all pallid and wet and useless, but I knew it didn't really matter that I'd embarrassed myself. Because the only thing Leah saw in that moment was someone who'd leapt up to make her favourite breakfast, and brought it to her in bed. I'm not sure exactly what I was trying to say with those pancakes, but I'm still saying it with every meal and lunchbox and glass of orange juice, some three years on.

Baby steps

It's funny how this sameness between food and love and care takes root. From the moment that we begin to split into two cells, then four, then eight, in our mum's womb, we begin to make her a part of us. She eats for us, she drinks and sleeps and breathes for us. The placenta – a heavy purple-grey mass of flesh, blood and magic – acts as a kind of clever middleman here, ferrying us all the nutrients from mum's food, the building blocks for life, via a gummy rope of umbilical cord and our fledgling belly button. We grow bigger, kick harder, until after nine months or so, we're ready to unceremoniously burst forth into the world.

We know plenty about this feeding relationship, between mum and *in utero* baby. It's what we're talking about when we say that someone is eating for two, or that 'the baby' is craving curry, or Quavers. It's why we steer clear of alcohol during pregnancy. When the time comes for us to be mums ourselves, we give and give and give, lending all of ourselves in order to create new life. This is the ultimate act of sharing: we share our food, nutrients, and even our bodies with this tiny fledgling human being. We give every scrap of love we have.

And every bite matters. For every mouthful of butter-glossed new potatoes that mum eats, baby is getting a taste for life outside. As babies, we also take mouthfuls of the amniotic fluid that our mum's body has made to cushion our stay in the womb. This amniotic fluid bears the imprint of all the things mum has eaten, so that before we've ever set foot in the world, we might have a taste for garlic, beef rendang, anchovies. After we're born, we lock onto any breast we can find, and begin to breastfeed: this milk, like amniotic fluid, is flavoured with the tastes of mum's food. We develop a discerning palate, and it's inextricably bound up with the foibles and fancies of mum. We are cute, tiny parasites, and we are eating for our lives.

I've framed this in terms of the relationship between mums and babies, but, of course, it can be anyone who shapes our tastes. Perhaps the parent who carried you to term is a transgender man, or perhaps they aren't comfortable with either 'mum' or 'dad' as a marker for their gender. Maybe your birth parent gave you a craving for curry, but you were raised in a meat-and-two-veg household. You might live with your grandad, with whom you cook and eat huge portions of rice and broth, or find solace in the familiar flavours of your auntie's apple pie. Although our tastes are shaped in the womb, and our hunger finds a voice the second we open our mouths to suckle, the way we eat is a patchwork of a million different people, circumstances and moments. In this patch-work, our families are key. They write the blueprint for a lifetime of gulping down as much food and love as we can stomach.

I often wonder how differently my life would have played out if I'd just been fed different food as a baby. I was the first of my parents' four children, and so was on the receiving end of more care, and food, than I knew what to do with. Because my mum and dad were such explorative eaters, that hunger was written into my bones: if not through the nuts and bolts of my DNA, then through the constant exposure to new flavours in those impressionable early years of my life, and the contagious excitement that rippled through our house every mealtime. I was fed blitzed up, low-salt versions of all the food my parents ate from when I was barely big enough to crawl. I ate spicy stews, curries and thick dal; I developed a taste for Oxo cubes, foraged from the kitchen cupboards, alluringly shiny in their little sweet-like wrappers (my parents were horrified). I smeared pasta sauce around my plastic plates and opened wide for spoonfuls of sweet-savoury dansak. I loved to eat, and sick up, little pots of fromage frais. All of this set me up for a lifetime of seeking out as many food thrills as I could: the sweeter, spicier, more potent, stranger, the better.

A full table

With four hungry kids in their charge, my parents had to work overtime to feed the family. As soon as the debris of one meal was cleared away, there'd be a tug at the hem of my mum's shirt and a little voice asking what was next, what was for dinner, and whether we could have a snack. It was a never-ending feeding frenzy, and mum and dad had to be smart to feed the six of us as well as possible, as quickly as they could and on the cheap. If dinner was a one-pot meal that cut down on washing-up, all the better.

The recipes that follow are some of the meals that we ate again, and again, and again. They're the easy midweek wonder dinners that can be whipped up in almost as little time as it takes a hungry family to polish them off. Of course, you don't have to have a gaggle of kids in your care to cook and enjoy these meals: they're as enticing to grown-ups as they are to little ones, and ideal if you have friends to feed or an impromptu group dinner to cater for. Don't get too precious about following my instructions, though – the whole point of these meals is that they're not supposed to be the kind of thing you need to go to the shop for. They're store-cupboard staples, to be tweaked, adapted or completely overhauled, however you please. These recipes all serve six (hungry) people.

Weeknight chickpea pasta with peppers and tomato

As a kid, I loved the sweetness of the peppers in this easy pasta dish. Chop four yellow, orange or red peppers into chunks, and throw into a large saucepan with a sliced onion, three crushed cloves of garlic and a couple of tablespoons of oil. Cook over a low heat with the lid on, stirring occasionally, until the pepper is perfectly tender. Add two tins of chopped tomatoes, two drained tins of chickpeas, a teaspoon of dried oregano, a teaspoon of smoked paprika, and a good pinch of chilli flakes. Simmer for 10 minutes. While the sauce cooks, boil 600g of pasta shapes in plenty of salted water – penne or fusilli work well, but truly this isn't Italy and nobody's going to report you to a *nonna* if you just use the mixed dregs of whatever pastas you have in the cupboard. Season the sauce with plenty of salt and pepper, drain the pasta, and mix the two together. We always used to beg for grated Cheddar with this, although frankly it is not necessary and it doesn't go. It's fun, though. Serves six.

Vegan chilli

No meat in this chilli means it's a lot cheaper than some of the more extravagant recipes out there, but the mix of beans, pulses and rice means it's just as filling as any authentic chilli con carne. Dice two onions, two carrots and two celery sticks, and cook over a medium heat with four tablespoons of vegetable oil in a deep, heavy saucepan. Put a lid on the pan and cook for 15 minutes, stirring occasionally, until the vegetables are starting to soften and sweat. Add two teaspoons of dried oregano, one teaspoon of ground cumin, one teaspoon of smoked paprika, one teaspoon of hot chilli powder, ½ teaspoon of ground cinnamon and three bay leaves. Fry for a few minutes before adding two tins of drained red kidney beans and a tin of chopped tomatoes. Stir in two tablespoons of tomato ketchup, 100g of long grain rice (rinsed and drained) and 750ml of vegetable stock. Bring to a simmer, then turn the heat down and cook for 40 minutes or so, stirring regularly to stop the rice from sticking on the base of the pan. If the sauce gets too thick, you may need to add another 100–120ml of stock as the chilli cooks. It's ready when the sauce is rich and thick, and the vegetables are tender. Season with plenty of salt and pepper, and serve with rice or jacket potatoes. Serves six.

Other people's houses

We don't know whether there's life elsewhere in the universe, or all the strange, beautiful creatures that lurk at the bottom of the ocean trenches. The overwhelming majority of existence is a mystery to us! We can't even hear very well, compared with a dog or a bat, or see all of the colours that there are to see. The world is full of secrets, and almost everything under the sun contains within it some new secret for us to discover. But there will never be anything quite as interesting, or as bizarre, as what goes on in other people's houses.

Mystery breeds curiosity, and that curiosity is what keeps us up into the small hours scrolling through the *Mail Online*'s 'Sidebar of Shame'. We love knowing the boring bits. This is why we fall over ourselves to know every last detail about Kim Kardashian's placenta pills, and red carpet pit stains, but scroll quickly past whatever charity project or landmine clearing or tiny orphans these stars might be involved with. That's not to say there's anything wrong with this fascination with the little things. In fact, I can't help but be suspicious of anyone who isn't a bit curious about Lupita Nyong'o's skincare routine. Do you think you can't do any better by your skin? Mate – who do you think you are?

This curiosity finds a particularly charged outlet when it comes to food. Despite the countless ways in which food is social and performative, there's still a big difference between the kind of eating that we do in public, and the eating that goes on behind closed doors – after midnight, in bed, in secret. The latter is endlessly interesting. After all, if we are what we eat, of course it's natural to want to get a slice of whatever richer, more attractive, more successful people are having. We're desperate to know what Laverne Cox puts in her smoothies, and how to eat our way to Nicki Minaj's butt. Even with rather less glamorous people, our food curiosity is keen. We peer into other people's trolleys at Aldi; we ask

Janine in the office what she's having for lunch every day. I am to this very day furious that every lunchtime I had to eat my school packed lunch with the lid artfully balanced over my curry, or couscous, or whatever, to shield it – and me – from the mingled curiosity and scorn of my friends, who were all sat there with cheese sarnies and Walkers. This very theory is what has made *Come Dine With Me* – a Channel 4 show where five people take turns to host dinner parties and say horrible things about each other, the food and their houses – so enduringly popular despite being really fundamentally pretty dreadful.

Because our eating habits are forged over such a long time, and across so many meals, plates, kitchen tables and places, we develop strange, deeply personal food quirks that bear the imprint of everything from that biryani mum ate while you were in the womb, to the Easter eggs you hoarded one spring when you were ten. These food habits might be perfectly normal to us, even though they make others gag. This is how people with mouths full of working teeth can drift along thinking it's perfectly normal to still cut off their crusts age thirty, or grown adults eat cornflakes soaked in orange juice. It's why I insist that my dad's spicy orange and bacon pasta is delicious even though it is, I suspect, objectively terrible.

I remember exactly how impressed and confused I was when I went round my friend Megan's house in year 5, and her mum made us spaghetti bolognese and put down a little bowl of grated Parmesan with a spoon in the middle of the table. What was this IMPRESSIVE TINY CHEESE and SPOON doing on the table? Why did it smell like feet? It was so delicious. I hadn't realised that having a trough of thickly grated Cheddar on the table, which we all dug into with our greedy little hands and threw over our bolognese with the care of farmers shovelling manure on the fields, wasn't how everyone necessarily ate their pasta. This was the first time

I realised that my family's funny way of doing things wasn't the only way, and that other families probably had strange dinner table traditions of their own. I was fascinated.

These debates never get tired. We happily pontificate and divide ourselves into little tribes, because each of these food idiosyncrasies is, we assert, an integral part of our approach to life. Are you a McDonald's or a Burger King person? Ketchup or brown sauce on a bacon sandwich? Do you have your scone with jam and cream, or cream and jam? What's your go-to order at Nando's? Do the Joneses all eat together as a family, or at their laptops? To dunk a biscuit in a cup of tea – yes or no? All of these things say as much about us as our fingerprints. And the answer to the last question is a decisive 'Yes', by the way.

Feeding the revolution

We don't really think of food as political. It feels wrong to talk about something so enmeshed with home, comfort and nostalgia as belonging in the realm of politics. We're used to relegating food to the domestic sphere: the kitchen and the place of women, a warm, familiar space far from the steeliness of legislation, government and war. So much of the language we use to describe food has soft edges: a warm scent, a round belly, a giddy indulgence. Food can't fight wars, and insofar as it feeds those who do fight them, it's as a stripped-back, macho kind of fuel – energy gels and protein packs that are nothing like the steaming plates of spaghetti and meatballs that fuel the home front.

When we talk about food and revolution, then, the conversation quickly turns to vapid evangelism. 'The Slow Food revolution is coming!' 'Make way for a revolution in pressure cooking!' 'This egg peeler will revolutionise your life!' But there *is* such a thing as revolutionary food. For as long as we've been fighting among ourselves, we've been using food as a tool to control, to subjugate, to nurture and to liberate. Far from the effete foodie world of mimosa brunches, kale shakes and craft beer, there's a part of food, and eating, that is revolutionary to its core.

Nineteen sixty-nine was the year of the Stonewall riots, the first military draft lottery since the Second World War and the moon landings: the whole political landscape of the United States was changing, and in the aftermath of the civil rights movement, racial tensions were fraught. It was an exciting, terrifying time. Everything was monumental – changes that flung us as far as the moon, or soaring through the sky in the first Boeing 747 – but in a church called St Augustine's in Oakland, California, progress took a different guise. Something vital, but mundane, was happening. Here, the Black Panther Party – the organisation that FBI Director Edgar J. Hoover called 'the greatest threat to the internal security of [the USA]' – did something truly radical: they launched a project feeding breakfast to local children.

While the more explicitly political side of the Black Panther Party, or BPP, dominated the headlines, their smaller, community-based programmes had been making amazing progress. The BPP was fighting hard for the lives of black people, in politics, in the community and by marching for justice. The people who formed the backbone of this organisation rallied against the complacency of the unengaged left and, rather than sitting back in comfort, took up arms in the fight against white nationalism and supremacy. This was ground-breaking resistance, but the community work and social charity going on behind the scenes was no less radical. Their so-called 'survival projects' included clothing distribution, the provision of free medical care, education and lessons on self-defence. They worked to aid drug and alcohol rehabilitation, and build sustainable community businesses.

The Free Breakfast for Children Program was perhaps the most successful of all these ventures, blossoming from the red walls of St Augustine's into a nationally deployed programme, feeding over 50,000 children at its peak. This was a programme that transformed the lives of children in deprived neighbourhoods who might otherwise have gone to school on an empty stomach.

In the face of neglect by the United States government, the activists of the BPP found a way to turn the focus back on the deprived communities that they came from, to nurture and support other black people. They recognised the power of food – not just the nourishment of the food itself, but also the social power of the act of serving and eating food together: the breakfast clubs were a forum for organisation, education and community bonding. It was a time when kids could get a square meal as well as food for thought. It was revolutionary action from the belly up.

As recently as 2011, 23.5 million Americans lived in food deserts: areas where large grocery stores are scarce, healthy food is difficult to come by, and incomes are low. In these areas – typically home to African-American populations, and often further isolated by poor infrastructure, neglect, and race-biased segregation of services – it's difficult to access healthy food, and pretty much impossible to eat well on a tight budget. It's shocking that even today, in Britain, there are people living in metropolitan areas and suffering from malnutrition, but it shines a light on why projects like the Free Breakfast for Children Program were so powerful. In a society that so unevenly distributes its resources, food scarcity disproportionately affects the most vulnerable communities, and so food distribution – in the form of soup kitchens, free breakfasts, meals on wheels, food banks – becomes a vital revolutionary tool.

Marie Antoinette allegedly precipitated the French

Revolution by decreeing, 'let them eat brioche!' Politicians now fall over themselves to be papped swigging a pint of real ale. 'I am one of you!' they say, 'I am the everyman!' When Donald Trump's government put forward a 'Muslim travel ban' in early 2017, one young Muslim woman became an internet sensation after heading to JFK airport with an armful of takeaway pizzas for the small army of people assembled there to protest the ban. Food can be a weapon! (And if you don't believe that food can be a weapon in the same way as a tank or a grenade, I can only assume you've never had the 4am finger buffet at Dempsey's Bar down Sheffield town centre.)

With the UK's largest food bank organisation, the Trussell Trust, having distributed over a million three-day emergency food supply packages in 2016/2017, food is clearly as political as ever. There's a temptation to hole yourself up in the kitchen as though in some kind of cocoon when the bad times hit. I know as well as anyone the draw to escapist food TV like *The Great British Bake Off*, or reruns of Nigella slinking around in her nightie. This kind of food is safe and cosy and nothing at all to do with the unforgiving world outside. There's enormous value to this aspect of food and cooking: this is what it is to have your waffle and eat it, too. Taking the time to treat yourself with kindness, and bask in the magnificence of all the wondrous tastes, sights, sounds and smells of the kitchen, is one of the most radical things you can do. This is self-care 101, nourishing your body and soul so that you can fight the good fight.

But we don't really have the luxury of only indulging in this softer side of food. In the wake of Brexit and Trump and every other political shitstorm heading our way, we have to be more vigilant, and more proactive, than ever. As well as nurturing ourselves, we need to turn our focus outwards to the world around us, and make the most of the revolutionary potential of food to change things for the better. Donate to a food bank next weekend. Research volunteer opportunities in soup kitchens near you, or cook a meal for an elderly neighbour. Help out with your local meals on wheels scheme, or even do something as small as just sharing your packet of Maltesers in the staff room. Feed the people around you. 'An army marches on its stomach,' Napoleon Bonaparte supposedly said. If that's the case, we'd better get cooking.

Having a Coke with you …

'… is even more fun than going to San Sebastian, Irún, Hendaye, Biarritz, Bayonne,' declared poet Frank O'Hara. He knew that what we eat together is worth a thousand big epiphanies or Michelin-starred solo meals or grand voyages. Here are some other things that are magical: picking the last of the season's fat, inky blackberries with you; eating toast in bed with you and arguing about the crumbs; reaching into the Minstrels packet at the same time as you and our hands grazing; unwrapping a cheeseburger with you; crying into cut onions with you; flipping pancakes with you and giving you the ones that aren't crumpled; walking home with a pocketful of Maltesers with you; cracking open the lid of the pan with you, and having the steam and the scent of dinner hit us both in the face; sharing my spoon with you; you.

Home cooking

Gagging on jellied eel

The smell of Southend seafront makes me feel ten years old again, careering along the beachside footpath in scuffed shoes with my friend Megan. It's a kind of air very different from the one I taste now, opening the window of my little house in Sheffield. Here, the wind has a light, clammy touch, sinking into the city from the Peaks; in Southend, the sea breeze dragged in the wet, heavy, saline smell of the mud flats. The sea would sweep in and pull out – lank ropes of seaweed, Coke cans and tiny discarded shells lagging behind in the mud – and then sweep in again so high that it lapped at the high sea wall. These smells – sharp saltwater, dank estuary mud, the tang of algae clinging to the beams of Southend pier – are the flavour of my own private Essex.

The Essex that most people think they know isn't a place to go to for good food. The flavour of Essex is, in the minds of many, the cloying sweetness of a glass of rosé wine at a sleek bar in Chelmsford, or the holiday-fresh smell of fake tan on the collar of a dress. And yet there is a whole wing of this misunderstood county that stretches out along the Thames like a phantom arm: it feels but is not felt, it has a flavour of its own that flows from Tilbury docks down through the scrubby flats of Benfleet, Leigh-on-Sea's cobbled streets of cockle sheds and the beach huts at Shoeburyness.

The River Thames, freed from the London rush, unbuttons

its shirt, spreads itself wide and slowly ambles this final thirty-odd miles to the sea. It's in this slower, tidal languor that the real flavours of estuary Essex come through. It's the flavour of shellfish coddled in the sheltered tidal waters, pots of shrimp and cockles. It's the wide-mouthed Essex drawl that comes out of our mouths, and the fish and chips that go in. Ice cream huts pepper the promenade, adding sweetness, while the rhythmic dollop, sizzle, shake and munch of the seafront doughnut kiosks sets the pace for slow seaside life. There are Chinese restaurants that hum with customers along the eastern stretch of the town, and hectic shops with Indian, Pakistani, Polish, Caribbean and East Asian foods clustered along London Road leading out of Southend town centre towards the capital. The flavour of a new Korean restaurant in the arches underneath the pier – the spots so long reserved for chequered tablecloth, sausage and chips, early bird special cafés (I thought long and hard about that 'é' and whether to include it or not, because really these places are caffs, not busied with affectations like little accents above the e) – is the flavour of Essex, too.

There is one place on the seafront that sells jellied eels in little polystyrene tubs – this is a flavour of Essex that I remember keenly, for better or worse. I was sixteen, and everything was stretched to the max: I pulled my curfew back, back, back until the tight leash that my parents kept me on was at breaking point; I tugged my jumper sleeves over my hands until every sweater and cardigan hung limp and distended; I picked at the edges of myself, getting as drunk and silly as I could while still retaining the capacity to drag myself home to bed; I danced along the boundaries of good taste in shorts so short they almost carved me in half. I was ready to stretch my stomach to its limits, too. I was going to – sat on the sea wall with my new friend Hayley, huddled together against the whip of the sea breeze – eat a cold pot of jellied eels.

I retched and I gagged. Tears came to Hayley's eyes. The eel sat heavy in my puckered mouth while the grey sea heaved in front of me. I heaved, too. It was wet and salty and slimy and everything that a closed-minded teenager would hate. I remember it, though, as clearly as I remember the crappy tubs of bargain ice cream I ate out the back of my friend's dad's pub, the 1p bubblegum balls I ate thirty a day of for the whole of year 6 (and which gave me two fillings in return), and the Scotch Bonnet chilli eaten in a burst of teen bravado, and washed down with two McFlurrys. The sea smell has got muddled with memories of Impulse body spray and Rolos and the smell of clean laundry, and all those timelines fold into one. But the tastes of my rambling, uncertain childhood stand clear even now, a decade on and 200 miles away. On anxious days, I swear I can still taste that jellied eel in my mouth.

Our memories are patchworks of taste. We might remember a particularly golden slice of lemon cake before we recall the birthday it celebrated, or be flung back to the fluttering happiness of being six years old by a bite of a Milky Way. A whole autobiography can be encoded in this or that food – an orange cake strewn with pine nuts on a June day, a place where you once ate a cheese pretzel the size of your head. My whole life – everything that's ever mattered to me – can be summoned to memory in a menu: chocolate cake with green frosting, red hot cinnamon sweets, Pom-Bears, ham and pickle sandwiches, a tin of Roses, instant noodles in pitta bread, cheese and onion pasty, mozzarella sticks, sweet potato doughnuts, pancakes with lemon and honey.

In *The Gastronomical Me*, food writer M. F. K. Fisher describes a defining memory of her own, the nostalgia lubricated and emboldened with the help of a belly of good food. Her first oyster came at the same time as a dance with a 'loose-limbed dreamy … seraphic' older girl. Whisked to the dancefloor in a flurry of silk skirts, she allows herself to be held in the girl's arms, while she holds the taste of the oyster in her mouth. The dizzy eroticism of the dance is an awakening; the oyster is a new frontier. 'Practically the Belle of the Ball I was! ... And with a dawning gastronomic hunger. Oysters, my delicate tastebuds were telling me, oysters are *simply marvellous!* More, more!'

These threads that link food and memory aren't just incidental. There are societal factors that make almost inevitable that food will make a cameo in your most vivid memories – not least the fact that we just cannot let an occasion (whether that's a wedding or the end of the working day) go by without using food as a celebratory, commemorative, compensatory tool. Whatever it is that you're remembering, there's a fair chance that there was some kind of food involved at the big moment. But there's also something happening on a far smaller scale, unfolding deep in the grey matter of our brains. Some people have speculated that perhaps this is thanks to the proximity of the area of the brain that deals with taste, to the hippocampus, where memories are formed. In a similar way, smells can be evocative because of the location of the olfactory nerves in relation to the hippocampus and the amygdala (which is involved with emotional learning) – these areas are so interconnected that brain injuries that affect memory can also lead to loss of smell.

It makes sense that our brains would mesh taste and memory together given the scariness of the world around us. The natural world is rich with danger, and every last toxic leaf and bug would have posed a threat to the lives of our hunter-gatherer forebears. When the stakes of trying something new from the menu are so high, the ability to remember food – good or deadly – is a potentially lifesaving skill. This kind of evolved survival technique isn't really something we rely on for our lives any more, but the capacity is still there in our minds. It means we zoom back to the 2008 school disco at a mere whiff of Lynx, or jet off to Tenerife with a waft of suncream. After all these years, it still transports me to Southend seafront on the back of jellied eel.

Salt beef and groundnut soup

There is a famous scene in a movie that I love, and it goes a little like this: two friends are sat across a table in a New York deli. The man orders salt beef on rye – a cinematic shorthand for his Jewishness. The woman, who isn't Jewish, asks for turkey on white bread, which functions as a kind of edible symbol of her all-American, W.A.S.P.-y identity. She wears this character in her blonde hair, too, and her primness, and her very un-New York uptightness, just as he follows nimbly in the well-trodden footprints of wisecracking, self-effacing secular Jewish characters before him. They are talking about the differences between men and women, and the social currency of sex, and whether a man would be able to tell if a woman was faking an orgasm. Maintaining that most women 'have done it at one time or another, so you do the math', the woman begins feigning a toe-curlingly awkward, fist-slamming, chest-heaving, gasping, shuddering, screaming orgasm. As she finishes the 'orgasm' and the whole restaurant sits in stunned silence, an older Jewish woman a couple of tables down pauses for thought, and addresses the waitress: 'I'll have what she's having,' she says.

Obviously, this scene from *When Harry Met Sally* is famous for a reason: it is fast and funny and wraps up with maybe the best one-liner in the whole of Nora Ephron's career. But the joke isn't just about gender any more than orgasms are just about performance: as Nathan Abrams explains in *Reel Food: Essays on Food and Film*, this scene is about culture and religion and goodness. It pulls together every single antithetical aspect of Harry and Sally's characters: his roguishness, her prissiness; his Jewishness, her W.A.S.P.-ishness; his lust, her restraint (and then her lust, his restraint). When the older woman at the nearby table says, 'I'll have what she's having,' she's pulling into focus the whole treacherous miasma of Kosher, desire and forbidden fruits. Sally is a blonde-haired, blue-eyed white Christian – she embodies both the epitome of socially endorsed 'desirability' and, for Harry, a disappointing slide away from the good Jewish girls that he might be expected to choose. She is exotic and attractive and very much not Kosher, and when she puts on her orgasmic display, she wears this strange sexiness bolder than ever. If the older Jewish woman wants what she's having, she's only mirroring the ambivalence of Harry himself, pulled towards the familiar old world, and this intriguing *tref* – non-Kosher – new frontier.

This interaction between food and identity is a familiar feature in films. Take the lobster in *Annie Hall*, for instance – a *tref* food wreaking havoc in Alvie's kitchen just as Annie wreaks havoc in his life. Or in *Big Night*, where Stanley Tucci's Secondo struggles to make concessions to an American market while keeping hold of his Italian heritage. What we eat is who we are, and we can assimilate or differentiate with food, clutch tight to our culture or transgress time-old rules. My grandad navigated an unconventional path through immigrant life by eating rice occasionally during his fledgling years in England, before forsaking Ghanaian food entirely in favour of an all-English menu of roast beef and potatoes, lamb and mint sauce, chicken and gravy.

I went to visit my grandad in hospital once. It was Sunday, I think. I travelled from London to Nottingham, and brought with me a get well soon card and a pack of pear drops, which were just boringly British enough that there was a chance this tiny, contrary, Ghanaian man might just like them. I sat by his bedside and said hello, but he didn't recognise me through bleary eyes. He huffed and rolled over, twisting his head as far away from me as he could. I knew I could reach out at that moment and tell him who I was, and that he would understand, be pleased and eat his pear drops. But I just sat still. He died on the Tuesday, and like any epiphany worth having I realised it then, two days late, that I needed to be brave and grab for the things that were mine. With the portal to my Ghanaian roots six feet under, I started learning about groundnut soup.

'GROUNDNUT SOUP,' began my aunt Esther's recipe. 'INGREDIENTS: SMOOTH PEANUT BUTTER E.G. 'SUN PAT', FRESH TOMATOES 4 OR ANY AMOUNT, ONION, FRESH PEPPER OR CHILLI POWDER, TOMATO PUREE, FISH OR CHICKEN OR MEAT, SALT.' I had asked Esther, my late grandad's niece, for help on making *nkatenkwan*, or groundnut soup, and this recipe arrived in the mail in an envelope marked special delivery. I had to sign for it on the doorstep, this little bundle of stapled papers containing a family tree, a recipe for groundnut soup and a reminder that I really should visit Esther in person if I wanted to learn properly. This remains to date the most Ghanaian thing that has ever happened to me.

Groundnuts are a staple of cooking across West Africa. This family of subterranean legumes includes peanuts – the only species readily available in the UK – but the groundnut umbrella extends also to the Bambara groundnut used in areas of south-eastern Nigeria, and little Hausa 'tigernuts'. In Ghana, groundnuts, specifically peanuts, are a staple part of many people's diets: peanut butter, roasted and salted peanuts, and peanut powder or flour all play a role in the country's cuisine. The crop, though spurned more recently by Western 'wellness' sorts for its alleged health risks, is everything that could possibly constitute a superfood: rich in protein, energy-dense and full of B vitamins, vitamin E and minerals such as magnesium and phosphorus. They are everything that is good in the world in a nutshell.

Groundnut soup, then, meant a lot to me as I tried to decipher the tastes of my heritage. Rich, savoury, uncluttered, earthy and hot, it stands miles apart from the bitty, plain, divided meals that Britain specialises in. Where we have full English breakfast and roast dinner and cold meat platters, Ghana has soups and stews and dense, chewy fufu dumplings. The flavours of the British Isles have firm outlines that trace the sea-shorn cliffs; Ghana's flavours seep across the plate and into Côte d'Ivoire, Benin, Togo and Nigeria in bright, bold strokes. We follow the beneficent instruction of Delia, to the minutest detail, where Ghanaians go straight to the font of all culinary knowledge, cradled safe in the hands of aunties up and down the country, guarded fiercely in special delivery envelopes.

The soup I make now is a little different from Esther's recipe, but I'm more than OK with this muddling: I've found a way to make this soup that works here, in Sheffield, and which bends to my tastes. Onions, garlic, ginger, Scotch Bonnet pepper, tomato purée, peanut butter and stock are the building blocks of the soup, although every time I make it, it shifts just a little – more spice, sweeter, richer, thicker. (Recipe on page 89.) There will be aunties who are appalled at this mixed and muddled *nkatenkwan*, but it works for mixed and muddled me: part British, part Ghanaian, these disparate lives coming together in the tangles of my hair and the ashy darkness of my skin when it hits the sun. Somehow, in this ever-changing bowl of peanut soup, I found myself with a memory of a home I have never been to, and a grandfather I barely knew. I eat in a deep bowl, flooded over fluffy rice, sprinkled with a fistful of salted peanuts.

Le Big Mac

We start trading foods when we're in the playground – a sweet for a crisp, a little bright blue globe of bubblegum for a yoghurt tube – and in one way or another, we keep on doing just this our whole lives. We use food as a bargaining chip and a bribe, bridging the gaps between our cultures. Breaking bread together is a symbolic coming together, just as clinking glasses is or letting a stranger bum a piece of gum. It's a million times easier to meet with a friend when there's a table laden with food between you. This interpersonal, intercultural fusion plays out in every borrowed recipe, bastardised classic and 'fusion' kitchen, bringing outsiders inside and sending the rest of us, in baby steps, to far-flung places. Food does the talking that words so often can't. To get a sense of how these kitchen syntheses happen, I want to look to an unlikely case study: McDonald's.

For many, McDonald's is shorthand for total globalisation. In this view of things, the whole world is melting into one homogeneous, grey lump. Globalisation is condensing all the richness of culture and diversity down to a single mass of big brands, slogans and multinational corporations, a lifeless hunk of money as dense as a neutron star. The worry is that these mega-companies will eventually manage to swallow every last local, native, small-scale business straggler, and re-forge the world in their image. The golden arches are a symbol recognisable in more or less any country in the world – even those where the fast food behemoth hasn't yet laid down roots. A Big Mac is a Big Mac is a Big Mac: this transnational sameness is uniquely comforting. What McDonald's allegedly stands for, to its critics, is a crusader for global Americanisation, flattening local food cultures to shadows of their former selves, and clearing out competition wherever it goes. But I'm not sure that it's all that simple.

Vincent: And you know what they call a ... a ... a
      Quarter Pounder with Cheese in Paris?
Jules: They don't call it a Quarter Pounder with Cheese?
Vincent: No man, they got the metric system. They
      wouldn't know what the fuck a Quarter Pounder is.
Jules: Then what do they call it?
Vincent: They call it a Royale with Cheese.
Jules: A Royale with Cheese. What do they call a Big
      Mac?
Vincent: Well, a Big Mac's a Big Mac, but they call it Le
      Big Mac.
Jules: Le Big Mac. Ha ha ha ha. What do they call a
      Whopper?
Vincent: I dunno, I didn't go into Burger King.

This exchange from the movie *Pulp Fiction* sums up the whole complex, counterintuitive duality of McDonald's. It is glocalisation – the twin pulls of global expansion (sameness, homogeneity and top-down supply) and local diversity (variety and tradition) – encapsulated in a single exchange. McDonald's, like all companies that operate across borders, recognises that from place to place, markets change: vocabulary, routine, tradition, taste and trust all vary, and so must the company. Le Big Mac™, then, is a tiny concession to the French language, while holding steadfast onto the recognisability (and bankability) of the 'Big Mac' name. The Royale with Cheese (actually Le Royal Cheese™) steers clear of imperial dogmatism, and translates itself for a metric French market.

And it's not just the McLanguage that shapeshifts as McDonald's finds its feet across the globe. In South Africa, the Boerie Double is a burger bun containing two boerewors-flavoured patties. The famous Sausage McMuffin is made of chicken sausage in predominantly Muslim Pakistan. Russian

McDonald's boasts some kind of battered prawn wrap, while in Thailand the popular apple pie has been reinvented with sweetcorn. These offerings aren't always as clear-headedly 'authentic' as you might expect – look at the Mexican influence on the McAloo Wrap with Chipotle Sauce™ in India, for example, or the gluten-free burger buns seen in carb-capital Italy, of all places. But they are small, playful and meaningful contributions to a population that is neither homogeneous nor static. Of course, the people of India want a McSpicy Paneer™. It makes sense that we in Britain want burger patties made from British and Irish beef. And why wouldn't the Filipino McDonald's franchise be entirely Filipino-owned?

We have bellies grumbling for the foods that are familiar to us – foods that have a place in the rituals and traditions of the societies that we belong to. When we are hungry for things, our appetites get written into the menus we eat. The golden arches may look the same wherever we go, but they're made of molten butter in France, mango flesh in India and the sunny glow of leche flan in the Philippines. The world is bigger and smaller than it ever was. It is more and less, the same and different. It is everything we want it to be, and it fills us with images of ourselves in the same mouthful as it nourishes us with otherness. This is the melting pot.

That's not to say that McDonald's isn't a deeply problematic company. It is huge, short-sighted, and, as its reach has trickled further around the globe, it has become a runaway train. Although the franchise makes efforts to cater to the tastes of locals, its heavy hand nonetheless squeezes the finer flavours out of our various food cultures. Some tastes are cemented into our national palate when McDonald's picks them up (our British taste for American-style double decker hamburgers is just one example), but other traditions – our penchant for a proper floury bap, or a nearly forgotten love of English mustard – have slipped out of favour, bulldozed by these catering giants. Just to be clear: the problem here isn't fast food (I love it!) or the growth of cheap restaurant chains (they're vital!); the issue is about tradition, and making sure that even when we're happily halfway through our Big Mac meal, we don't completely forget the *doro wot*, or *ackee*, or Yorkshire puddings that made us.

I am the sugar

The culinary imperialism encapsulated in the McDonald's global conquest isn't anything new. Look at tea, for instance. Tea is as British as grass-stained cricket whites and the Women's Institute. It seeps into the cracks between Brighton pier and The Streets and Gogglebox; it oils the heavy cogs of the day. Our eating rhythms are so steeped with this tea fanaticism that it colours the very fabric of our national identity: we're a nation of tea drinkers – polite, tooth-stained, just-so – whether that's a Sports Direct tankard of the stuff or a barely-there porcelain teacup. A cup of tea can stand for manners, properness and goodness, or the opposite of all these things, depending on when, where and how it comes. A posh colleague once wrote in a less than favourable report that I'd given her a 'builder's brew', which I knew was about a lot more than just tea.

And yet in spite of this taste for tea, and all the sense of self anchored in the muddy waters of this drink, it's not really ours at all. 'I did send for a cup of tee (a China drink) of which I never had drank before,' commented Samuel Pepys in his diary some 350 years ago. Tea was a strange, new import steadily finding a foothold. It was foreign and 'exotic', shipped hundreds of miles across the seas from China at a time when many people's beverage of choice was good English ale. Tea was as un-English a drink as could be imagined – as novel to the British palate as the Hawaiian poké bowl craze is today. But within a century, tea had become England's favourite drink. Its popularity trickled down from royalty to aristocracy to the salons of the middle classes, until tea was a drink for the masses.

This boom in the tea market was astronomical, and it was in no small part thanks to another exciting new import: something that made tea more palatable, sweet and nourishing by the spoonful. The key to tea was sugar. Sugar had been available in England in one form or another since the Middle Ages, when it had been introduced to Europeans by Arabic traders. Along the banks of the River Jordan, sugar cane was grown by Muslim traders, who then sold their sugar via Venice and Genoa to cold, northern Europe. Although sugar was for a long time an expensive delicacy – used more like a spice or seasoning than an ingredient in its own right – it wasn't long before production techniques and trade routes made sweetness a popular commodity. Renaissance cooks took to sugar with the overzealous excitement of a kid in a candy shop, dredging everything from meat to pasta with the sweet stuff. Honey was ousted as the nation's sweetheart, and by 1554, London played host to the UK's first sugar refinery. Just like tea, sugar slowly seduced the wider population, and these two young upstarts became partners in crime: the tea boom fuelled the market for sugar, and the sugar surge enabled tea to really take off.

The trouble is, neither tea nor sugar were things that, at the time at least, could be produced in the UK. It was colonial missions to the Americas and Caribbean that established the sugar plantations that allowed traders to meet demand for sugar, and thus bring prices down. These plantations would never have been possible without the labour of thousands and thousands of slaves. The Dutch, Portuguese and British were all involved in this bloody trade, both in the establishment of these sugar plantations and in their continuing, blossoming hunger for the products of that slave labour.

Tea, meanwhile, had its own morally questionable empire. In the early 1700s, the East India Company established a customs-free trade deal with the Mughal emperor in Bengal; within a century, it had established a virtual monopoly over all trade in India, including the trade in tea. The company expanded its reach way beyond just commodities and started seizing land, communities and, indeed, entire empires, with a private army double the size of the British army. It succeeded in dissolving the Maratha empire and taking great swathes of India. So talented were we at the art of pillaging that we even stole the Hindustani slang word 'loot' – rarely heard in Britain before the reign of the East India Company – to describe the very act of plunder. The polite clink of spoon on teacup, the rattle of saucers, the delicate pouring of tea: these things were the faintest, politest, whispered echoes of the bloodshed raging across the seas.

Tea with sugar is a blood sport. It is a cup of colonialism brewed strong with the labour of other people, in other places, drowned out by the sound of our tea morning chatter. It is true that the processes by which tea reaches us have changed – they've come a long way from their murderous roots (there's even a tea plantation in Cornwall now, and a lot of sugar is derived not from tropical sugar cane but local sugar beet). But the history of tea and sugar casts a long shadow over this supposedly genteel tradition, and it's a history we owe it to everyone to look at. If the cup of tea is the quintessential British drink, what does that say about the forces that made us? Cultural theorist Stuart Hall was born in Jamaica and spent much of his adult life studying and working in England. As a black man whose life stretched across these two disparate cultures – from a nation that was, in the mid-eighteenth century, one of the world's biggest sugar producers, to a nation that forged a colonial empire – he had a lot to say on the power of tea and sugar in the identities we assume.

> People like me who came to England in the 1950s have been there for centuries; symbolically, we have been there for centuries. I was coming home. I am the sugar at the bottom of the English cup of tea. I am the sweet tooth, the sugar plantations that rotted generations of English children's teeth. There are thousands of others beside me that are, you know, the cup of tea itself. Because they don't grow it in Lancashire, you know. Not a single tea plantation exists in the United Kingdom. This is the symbolization of English identity – I mean, what does anybody in the world know about an English person except that they can't get through the day without a cup of tea?

The tastes we have aren't necessarily grown in the earth we plant our toes in. British appetites aren't made of nettles and brambles and vole, but of crumbling dark brown sugar from Brazil, flanks of fat-rippled Norwegian salmon and maize from across the Atlantic. Some of these flavours are sweet because they drift naturally onto our palates, others leave a bad taste in the mouth with their imperialist roots. When we consume things that are stolen, we're consuming the bodies, money and livelihoods of the people we stole from. And when the foods we take such joy in cause suffering for others, it's only so long before they start to rot us from the teeth out.

It's tempting to think we're all well beyond this kind of culinary imperialism now, and in many senses we are. Our streets are filled with stores stocking Polish, Indian, Iranian and Jamaican groceries, markets have vendors selling food inspired by places from Manila to Mississippi. In spite of the inconsistency in print book sales in recent years, cookbooks continue to sell well, at least in part down to the popularity of increasingly specialised regional cookery books. Where Elizabeth David's *A Book of Mediterranean Food* might once have been sufficiently specific, we now have books about Sichuan cooking, Palestinian food or recipes from Catalonia. Even the supermarkets have diversified their offerings, catering not just to established and immigrant communities but also to fantasies of far-off lands: the power of our culinary curiosity fuels a demand for kimchi, for example, that balloons way beyond the appetite of Britain's comparatively small Korean community.

By and large, we Brits want to know as much about different places as we can, but in our quest to try China in a mouthful, or taste Israel over brunch, many of us end up seeing the rest of the world through the diffracting, blurry, distorting lens of a bowl of soup, an apple slice, a mug of *kombucha*. The result is a myopic, romanticised vision of otherness, which fetishises different cuisines rather than engaging with the cultures that created them, or raids them for appealing window-dressing. My Singaporean friend was once offered an 'authentic Asian experience' by a white waiter in a white-run pan-Asian pop-up in east London. I've heard countless stories from people of colour about their friends, boyfriends and colleagues who profess to finding their culture 'fascinating', and by the way they 'really *love* bubble tea/ackee/dosa [delete as applicable]'. We can heal all kinds of wounds and communicate in any language when we talk with food, granted, but this doesn't really go further than tongue-deep if it doesn't come hand in hand with actual dialogue, listening and respect.

What's more, the portraits of other cultures that we see through food aren't necessarily accurate. At what point does a homage to Mumbai's cuisine become a parody? And in whose hands are treasured Iranian recipes truly authentic? Lorraine Chuen, who writes the blog *Intersectional Analyst*, found in early 2017 that almost 90% of 'Chinese' recipes in *The New York Times* food section were authored by white people. For 'Vietnamese' recipes, white authorship comes in at 95%. African food is often treated as a single entity, again with overwhelmingly white bylines. On blogs and social media, people often share pictures of, for example, Filipino food posed with chopsticks (a weird meshing of very different East Asian cultures, because Filipinos largely eat with spoons and forks) or Ethiopian food styled against a backdrop of Ghanaian kente cloth.

These things aren't necessarily terrible in and of themselves – these confusions happen naturally when one culture looks to another for inspiration. Not everyone can know everything about every other culture, and it's easy to get it wrong when you don't. However, these sins of ignorance are still (at best) irritating and even actively harmful to others, and they often spring from a worrying gap between the culture we actually inhabit and the one we feel like seeing. If you're white British, you can choose not to notice Britain's background of colonialism and imperialism, the sections of its society who expound xenophobia and intolerance of other cultures, and the continued pay gap between white workers and people of colour. If you're not white British, you might not be able to ignore this so easily. Viewed within this context, it's not hard to see why a Thai person in Britain would hold tight to their cuisine in the face of a white-run food truck peddling just the same (or worse!) stuff for double the price under the banner of 'authenticity'. It's also not hard to imagine how someone might be miffed at wellness bloggers reinventing turmeric milk (a common drink for some in India) as some 'immune-boosting' miracle food and selling it at £4.50 a pop.

The real question isn't about what we eat, but *how* we eat. Eating well is about eating with due deference. It means giving credit to those who deserve it, and not just sweeping

blithely through the world on a kitchen tablecloth magic
carpet. We can eat as much Pakistani food as we want, make
it at home according to some Nigella recipe, and mangle the
dish to adapt it to our own tastes. In Meera Sodha's recipes,
there are frequent references to foods from the Lincolnshire
she grew up in: fat Lincolnshire sausages find their way into a
potato curry, a courgette glut inspires spiced courgette koftas.
My Norwegian friends insist that tacos are a kind of adopted
national dish. Even potatoes – as homely and 'normal' as
British and Irish foods get – were once alien imports from the
Americas. In southern Italy, sultanas speak to the influence of
historical Arabic trade links, while in Surrey's commuter-belt
countryside, a burgeoning wine-producing culture is taking
root. Food writer Soleil Ho (who also co-hosts the *Racist
Sandwich* podcast) once wrote about the taste of immigrant
life: 'Maggi seasoning, rice noodles, and fish sauce [were]
ingredients that, to a Vietnamese-American, could make
even a piece of Wonder Bread taste something like home.
When I learned more about Vietnamese cuisine, I was surprised to learn that dishes I loved, like nui ga (chicken soup
with rotini) or banh mi on sliced white bread, didn't exist in
Vietnam.' All this culinary politics of difference and assimilation finds form in artist Hayley Silverman's tiny sculptures
of soup bowls, which come to life with little figurines: a crew
of miners, a mother and son playing piano. These are portraits of the sloppy, surreal, tantalising cultural landscapes of
her home in New York City.

Spending your money at local restaurants and takeaways
owned by people from those cultures is a good start. We
need to keep our restless fingers from clicking on headlines
like 'You won't believe what weird foods they eat in China!',
and wind our necks in if we're tempted to comment on a colleague's 'ethnic' food. If we want to establish a food business
that adopts the cuisine of a culture that isn't our own, we ought

to make sure we consult, employ and provide for the people whose culture we are borrowing from. (For instance, if you are white, don't open a 'Bangladeshi' food truck in Whitechapel unless you're willing to price your food in line with the spending power of the Bangladeshi community that lives there.) Most of all, we should rethink the lines that divide what is plain from what's 'strange': see all the bizarreness of our familiar foods (think hard-boiled eggs, wrapped in sausagemeat, covered in bread and deep fried), and look closer to see the wonder in foods we're less used to, like blood soup, chicken's feet and Florentine-style tripe. The power to resist the outdated, inward-looking, xenophobic narratives about 'good' and 'bad' food exists right here, in our bellies and our mouths. Food is a political thing, and that's half the magic of it.

Cookbooks

When I was away at university, I had a very small collection of cookbooks that I read like novels each night in bed. I dipped into Dan Lepard's *Short and Sweet*, entranced by the descriptions of apple, walnut and custard cake, brown sugar chocolate cake and panettone teacakes. He took the spoon from my hand when I was baking tired and frustrated in a late-night bakeathon, shoved the cake in the oven and seemed to say to me: 'This will come out lopsided and imperfect and you're gonna love it anyway.' Nigella Lawson whispered in my ear as I stood over the hob in my rat-infested flat in Kilburn, telling me all about coffee mornings and Bundt cakes and all manner of delicious bougie things from a life that was completely alien to me. I devoured *The Flavour Thesaurus* like it was a glossy mag. I fell asleep thinking of dark chocolate chunk cookies made with olive oil, saffron risotto, butter-fried sea bass and treacle tart, rolling the syllables slowly around my mouth.

Cookbooks have lots of advantages over novels for fuelling your dreams: first, there's a gross charm to food splatters and stains and sticky bits in the pages of cookbooks, that no margin scribble could ever match. Second, recipes are short – these are psalms for the ungodly, little doses of goodness in the most bitesize chunks. Third, the very nature of a cookbook means it's a glance into a coveted life, and a literal instruction manual on how to seize a bit of that joy for yourself. Any cookbook worth its salt isn't just a dry how-to, it's an immersive, bossy, companionable, seductive thing. A good cookbook is a friend in the kitchen.

And the way people talk about their favourite cookbooks really *is* as though they're conjuring the names of old mates: 'Ottolenghi does this' or 'Meera Sodha says this is the *only* way'. We over-familiarly chat about Jamie, Nigella or Delia as though they were childhood sweethearts of ours, and somehow their influence bleeds into every last crack in our lives. Knowingly or otherwise, we mould ourselves in their image. At one point during university I was so deep in this recipe worship that Nigel Slater became Nigel, and Nigel became God. He was the kindly, indulgent (maybe *too* indulgent), slightly rude, completely minted uncle I had dreamed of, and I honestly couldn't think of anything I wanted to do in this short life more than make him proud. I've been to therapy since and it's all making sense how the gentle words of a distant man turned into the edicts of a towering father figure in my mind, but that's a story for another day. I can't help it, but I still hear his voice occasionally if I'm cutting bananas or rye bread or carrots. 'Ruby,' he whispers with the slightest of lisps, 'cut it ever so thin. The thickness of a pound coin should do.'

This isn't about Nigel Slater, though. Different people have different styles of cooking, and one woman's Nigel/God is another woman's salmonella. There are wonderful food writers whose voices I can't stand, and terrible ones who I'd trust with my life. Kardashian-Jenner clan matriarch Kris Jenner has a cookbook with anecdotes about her home life and her children, and it nourishes every strand of me, but perhaps you like your cooking teachers to be more matronly and to the point. I must be the only food writer in the country who has never read Elizabeth David or Jane Grigson (shame on me), but ask me about Chrissy Teigen's *Cravings* or the recipe cards my mum keeps in a raggedly little box, and I could bore you witless.

Whoever you click with, the real joy of having these worldly, wordy friends in the kitchen is that they fend off the loneliness that it's so easy to feel when we cook alone for ourselves. They crawl out of the dog-eared pages of our old cookbooks, hoist themselves onto the kitchen counter and softly, but authoritatively, give us permission to treat ourselves to something that tastes good. A tin of chickpeas won't do, and a plate of unbuttered, unseasoned pasta is no fit dinner: they remind us that our bodies can soak up all the blissful sensations of the world, and they tell us how to get there. There's a line in *Sex and the City* where Carrie says that she used to buy *Vogue* instead of dinner when she first moved to New York – 'I found it more nourishing.' Sometimes, when the fridge is bare and it's late, I turn to recipes for this sustenance and feed my soul. Here are three recipes inspired by the lessons I've learned from my favourite cookbooks.

'More is more' caramel swirl brownies

My parents had a copy of the *Hamlyn New All Colour Cookbook* and I remember, more clearly than I remember my first bike ride, holiday or day at school, how I used to lounge across the floor with it, poring for hours over the things I wanted to eat. There were little snowmen covered in desiccated coconut, jam tarts and a birthday cake with rugged spikes of green icing and little chocolate figures. I'm pretty sure there was some kind of lamington that I particularly fancied, and even a syrup-drenched sponge. These recipes set me up for a lifetime of a 'more is more' mindset, and an insatiable sweet tooth. Little did I know at five or six years old that, fifteen years down the line, I would somehow find my way onto a cooking show with the author of that book – some woman, Mary Berry, whose name meant nothing to me at the time. These brownies channel that 'more is more' spirit into sweet and sticky caramel brownies.

Preheat the oven to 180°C/fan 160°C/gas mark 4. In a small saucepan over a low heat, gently melt 150g of unsalted butter. Remove from the heat before whisking in 100g of soft dark brown sugar and 200g of tinned caramel (the Carnation stuff that you can find alongside the condensed milk on the supermarket shelf – don't use 'real' caramel because it'll be far too sickly!), just until well mixed. Beat in two eggs, 100g of plain flour, 30g of cocoa powder and a quarter of a teaspoon of salt. Chop 75g of white chocolate into chunks, and break 50g of walnuts into bite-sized pieces. Stir these into the brownie batter. Pour the mixture into a 15×22cm baking tin, lined with baking paper. Dollop little spoonfuls (100g in total) of caramel over the top, then use a knife to lightly ripple the caramel through the batter. Sprinkle with another 25g of white chocolate chunks and bake for 20–30 minutes (note it's better to under-bake than over-bake!). Makes 9–12 brownies.

Fish tacos with crunchy red cabbage and fennel

Relish isn't strictly a recipe book, but a graphic novel: a memoir, via food, about the author Lucy Knisley's life. When it comes to food, Lucy is independent, single-minded and stubborn, but despite this culinary intrepidity (which I related to), it was the ways that food brought people together, smoothed over the rifts between them and bartered for a place in their hearts that really mattered in the end. It made me want to leave behind the detached, semi-intellectualised ways in which I'd grown used to thinking about food, and throw myself back into the cluttered, sociable, shared kitchen. Food is about people, and this recipe is perfect for cooking with people – divide and conquer the component parts (four parts, four people) and it'll be on the table in no time.

Someone needs to take charge of the tortillas. Mix 300g of plain flour with a quarter of a teaspoon of salt and two tablespoons of corn or vegetable oil in a mixing bowl. Slowly add 150ml of warm water, working the dough with your hands until it comes together in a smooth mass. Cover with cling film and leave to rest. After half an hour or so, the dough will have relaxed enough that you can roll it. Divide into twelve pieces and roll them out on a floured surface into circles roughly 15cm across.

While the sous chef rolls the tortillas, another person can start frying them one by one. Set a dry frying pan over a medium heat and cook for 30–60 seconds on each side. They should be spotted with brown and cooked through. Set the cooked tortillas aside.

A third person can work on getting the salad together: very finely slice a quarter of a red onion, 100g of red cabbage and one bulb of fennel, then toss with one teaspoon of corn or vegetable oil, two teaspoons of lime juice and a generous sprinkle of salt.

Meanwhile, put another person to work preparing the fish. Into a little bowl, put two teaspoons of smoked paprika, half a teaspoon each of cayenne pepper, salt, ground cumin and cocoa powder, and a quarter of a teaspoon of cinnamon. Dice 450g of white fish, such as pollock, haddock or coley, into 2–3cm cubed pieces. Toss the fish in the spice mix and fry in a little oil over a medium heat for 4–6 minutes, until browned all over and cooked through.

All the components can finally come together now. Lay out the tortillas, fish and salad on the table along with a little pot of sour cream and a lime cut into wedges. Assemble the tacos – if there are four of you, you can have three each – and enjoy.

Oaty brown sugar soda bread

There's a chapter in Laurie Colwin's *Home Cooking* where the author (she's American) reminisces about English food. She describes things that I'd scarcely even noticed, through curious virgin eyes. Through this lens, things as mundane as eggs, fudge and roast dinners became new and wonderful. I found myself thinking about Cheddar and polystyrene cartons heavy with chicken shop fries. I realised that I was in love with Rowntree's fruit pastilles and sachets of Angel Delight, and took to every shopping trip as though I was surveying some brave new world. Needless to say, I was smitten with the book. This easy bread takes things that are abysmally dull (especially compared with the technicolour palettes of Mediterranean kitchens) and gives you the chance to magic up something magnificent from them.

Preheat the oven to 180°C/fan 160°C/gas mark 4. Combine 200g of wholemeal flour, 50g of rolled oats, one tablespoon of dark brown sugar, three-quarters of a teaspoon of bicarbonate of soda and a quarter of a teaspoon of salt in a large bowl. Stir in 60g of full-fat Greek yoghurt and 100–125ml of water – just enough to bring the dough together to a soft, slightly sticky mass (it's important that it's not too dry and rubbery, or it won't rise). Form into a rough cob shape on a greased baking tray, sprinkle with some more oats and score a cross in the top with a sharp knife. Bake for 50 minutes, then leave to cool slightly before serving with salted butter and jam – blackcurrant jam on this bread is the stuff dreams are made of. Makes one small loaf.

Digested: Food on film

I talk a lot about film when I talk about food. Even though the red carpet is a million miles away from the dining table, food and film feed into one another in ways we might not expect. We scoop up fistfuls of salty popcorn while we drink in images from the silver screen; we sink into nostalgia with mouthfuls of a favourite meal as much as we do by watching a movie we know by heart; taste and smell (ice-cold Fanta, a share bag of M&Ms) ground us in the here and now, anchoring our bodies while cinema pulls our minds to far-off places. And the food we see within films is, more often than not, a vital narrative tool: amid all the action, drama, gore and sex of the screen, the act of eating is something that helps us relate to the strange, often sinister characters we see in front of us. Cinematic meals are morality tales, grim portents, innuendos, charades, connections and cues. These vignettes are the whole of food, eating, life and hunger in a few shimmering frames. Here are some of my favourites.

I've already talked all about how much I love Nora Ephron (pages 111–13), but there's no such thing as too much Nora, and I just have to tell you about Julie & Julia. Food was always there in Nora Ephron's work, but in Julie & Julia it stepped out of the supporting cast and into the spotlight. It's based on the real-life Julie Powell's blog that charts her attempts to cook her way through TV chef superstar Julia Child's oeuvre over the course of a year. The film is full of the most sumptuous shots of French food: sole meunière brought to the table still sizzling in its pan, browned butter rippling around the tender flesh; a bowlful of chocolate cream pie filling, velvety and thick; butter; more butter. This is a film about the joy of cooking as much as it is about eating. It is about the process of cooking, and the passion that drives that process, and this is nowhere more evident than in what is, for me, the most poignant scene in the film when Julie, having spent so many months living and breathing the work of Julia Child, her own life curving to follow Child's unlikely path, is roundly snubbed by Child. In an instant, the reverie snaps, and the mythic, magnificent Julia Child disappears, replaced by the grouchy, human, slightly less palatable real person. This is the whole of the saga of cooking: putting all of yourself into a pan, sweating it out, changing the very fibres of you, only to realise when it comes to the tasting that it's gone sour, and curdled, and the dream has burnt onto the bottom of the pan. This is real food.

In the Oscar-nominated Chocolat, the focus is on magic and mysticism, and all the alchemical wonder that food can contain. In it, Juliette Binoche's Vianne sets up a chocolaterie where, contrary to the studied seriousness that we expect from French cooking, each chocolate is an imperfect, indulgent and decidedly feminine exercise in generosity. Every truffle is plump with schemes to enrich some person's love life or revitalise another's. Each praline has a story. Even the method of selection is whisked, with a flurry, from the hands of the customer and turned into a game: the spin of a wheel, a fuzzy shape seen in the spinning patterns, and a perfect chocolate for you, magicked from the pregnant shadows of the shop. It's a wondrous place, and it exists in defiance of the conservative values of the village where it sits. Vianne's mother, we learn, came from a spiritual, travelling people. She blew in on the wind and left just as quick. Her dad, on the other hand, was a pharmacist. And from this unlikely mix, of buttoned-up *propriety, wilfulness, science and spirit, comes Vianne, the* chocolatier, *pure gold – rebelliously sweet, unapologetically feminine, in a serious, patriarchal world.*

Turn to My Big Fat Greek Wedding *and food plays a different role: it is a real, tangible extension of all the verbal gags that pepper the film – a way of contrasting Greekness with non-Greekness, giving a material form to the differences between Greek Toula and all-American fiancé Ian. In one scene where Ian meets Toula's extended Greek family, it comes out that he is a vegetarian. 'Oh that's OK!' exclaims Aunt Voula, 'I make lamb!' In another scene, Ian's parents arrive at the Portokalos house with a Bundt cake, which matriarch Maria accepts and uses as a plant pot holder. These are the same kind of cross-cultural faux pas that I mentioned play a role in* Annie Hall *and* When Harry Met Sally *(pages 133–4).*

Another popular trope in food-centric films is the dethroning of the critic. This is the world of the underdog, or the under-rat in the case of Pixar's Ratatouille, *in which a family of gourmand rats turn around the fortunes of a struggling Paris restaurant. At just one taste of a perfect ratatouille – not one made with expensive equipment or riding the back of a Michelin star, but a hand-crafted meal, made with love – the proud, impossible critic softens and yields to the pure pleasure of the food. And as viewers, we couldn't be happier. We want to see joy and flavour and happiness win the day, and so we rally against the homogenising, stifled tastes of the critic. It's a gastronomic uprising.* Mystic Pizza *feels very similar. In this coming-of-age classic, we follow the successes and stumbles of a group of friends through their last summer in their hometown before they split for college. At the heart of the girls' stuttering, weaving, unsteady stories is a humble pizza restaurant, and the ascetic, make-or-break judgement of local critic, 'The Fireside Gourmet'.*

Of course, there's no talking about food and fantasy without mentioning Roald Dahl, and the many film adaptations of his books. In the 1971 Willy Wonka & the Chocolate Factory, *there is liquid chocolate mixed by waterfall, and fizzy lifting drinks that carry you higher, and higher and higher. But this isn't pure saccharine loveliness – this is no Enid Blyton picnic with ham and teacakes and lashings of ginger beer. In Roald Dahl's gastronomical paradise, there's always a bite. It comes towards the end of a mouthful, slyly, gleefully creeping along the tongue, over the lips and outwards into a mischievous smirk: candies that turn you into a huge, swollen blueberry, and experiments that shrink you so small that you could be crushed underfoot.*

Funnily enough, though, Willy Wonka & the Chocolate Factory, *and the book it's based on, isn't even really about the magic of food or eating or cooking. It's about the frenzy and hysteria that descend when people begin buying Wonka bars, clamouring for a Golden Ticket. It's about what happens when Augustus Gloop succumbs to illicit, insubordinate greed, and how a single chocolate bar can light up a little boy's day. It's about whether your gluttony will make you into a 'bad nut', and whether you can keep your head in the face of a psychedelic, marvellous landscape of sweet temptation. This is a sweet-toothed fable for the modern child.*

There are dozens of other films I could mention with their own unique outlooks on food and appetite. There's the old lady spooning meatballs into Adam Sandler's outstretched palm in The Wedding Singer, *an embodiment of maternal (over)protection. Or all the feasts of Hayao Miyazaki's* Howl's Moving Castle *or* Spirited Away. *Baking stands for steadiness, homeliness and love in a gaggle of romantic comedies, from* Stranger than Fiction, *to* It's Complicated, *and* The Perfect Man. *Food is bribery and greed in* The Lion, The Witch and The Wardrobe, *and the pursuit of perfection in the Japanese films* Sweet Bean *and* Jiro Dreams of Sushi. Babette's Feast *is about single-minded determination, while* Chef *studies what happens when that pride sends us astray.* Tampopo *examines our entire relationship with food to encapsulate pretty much all of these themes at once. In every one of these films, whether food is at the heart of the story, or just a telling detail, it is larger than life, and no matter what your opinion of the film itself, your hunger's bound to be awakened. Watch them with popcorn in hand.*

Bad taste

Junk

The chaos and clamour of an open kitchen: a regiment of cooks in crisp uniforms slip from one counter to another, building each order like a Lego kit – bun, patty, gherkin, cheese, stacked in turn. I idle my thumbs across my grubby phone screen while I wait for the food to be ready. But faster than I check my texts, the meal is there, tessellated snug with the composition of a Renaissance painting, fries spilling towards my drink, drink standing tall alongside the smart, squat burger. When I open the burger paper, there is always a nugget of warm, golden cheese that has lost its way and stuck to the waxy paper wrapper. Before I do anything else, I scrape this cheese off with my finger and let it melt on my tongue. I take a bite of the burger, and exhale all the tangles of stress from my chest – the bun is sweet and soft, the meat full of savour, the gherkin perfectly sharp. Every flavour is choreographed to tug at whatever part of the brain controls total and utter bliss. I am in heaven in Burger King.

But what thanks do we give the everyday, unromantic, miraculous fast foods that routinely save our bacon following a long day at work, or scrape our morale off the floor the morning after the night before? There is as much magic in a box of salt and pepper chips, curry sauce and a can of Rubicon Mango as there is in any 'evocative', 'masterful' Heston Blumenthal-designed meal. I believe as fully in the restorative powers of potato waffles and fried egg on my health as I do in nine-hour sleeps. There's a unique beauty to the ballet that is the mechanics of McDonald's, or Burger King, or KFC, and the way that steaming hot food can appear, from nothing, in front of you for just a couple of quid.

The chasm between haute cuisine and 'junk' has never yawned so wide. Up soaring with the clouds is the cult of celebrity chefs – cooks who started in the brimstone heat of the kitchen and somehow got elevated to the ranks of culinary gods, with restaurant chains, pasta sauce ranges, magazine covers. These so-called savants tread in the overwhelmingly white, male footsteps of every other gastronomic genius that came before, sanding down the fuzzy edges of home cooking, making a virtue of exclusivity, and pulling food as far away from its nurturing essence as possible. Occupying a densely populated middle ground are the TV cooks and food writers, straddling the gap between the restaurant and the kitchen table. There's a sense of goodness, almost self-righteousness, about this group (of which I'm undoubtedly a part). Their cooking is peppered with the presumption that home cooking is not only pleasurable, but infused with a kind of moral good: cook from scratch to avoid an early death; show who you really are in a jar of homemade onion chutney.

And languishing in the muddy waters of low culinary culture is fast food, junk food, processed food, packaged food. Ready meals, takeaways, packets of Hobnobs, frozen foods, tins of potatoes, cheap and fatty cuts of meat, bargain buckets, spaghetti hoops, instant custard, jars of pre-made pasta sauce, instant noodles, white sliced bread, chocolate bars, fizzy pop and heavy, steaming polystyrene trays of donner meat and chips all fall under this umbrella. They stretch across every nutritional group, from protein-packed baked beans to energy-dense pork shoulder. What's more, they're delicious: when you eat a chip butty, glistening with salt and cut with vinegar, the whole world folds softly around you like a velvet blanket; a sip of a Wimpy milkshake will make your jaw throb and your tastebuds sing; a microwaved shepherd's pie meal will take you to holy mass on a Wednesday night.

Most of all, though, they are cheap. There are no gate-keepers here: no cover charge, advance booking, expensive ingredients, dress code, pomp, ritual or hefty bill. These are the most democratic foods we have, open to anyone, on more or less any budget, no matter the demands of work, child-care, ill health or poverty. The only thing definitively linking all of these 'junk' foods is that they're available, convenient and affordable, and therefore popular. Maybe the reason that all these vastly different foods are lumped together in one rubbish category isn't because of their quality or nutritional value, but precisely because they are the foods of the people. In a society where anybody can afford a steak bake and a can of Coke, the goalposts for aspirational eating are forced to move to classier things.

Fast food – and I mean the likes of Burger King, not Gourmet Burger Kitchen or some similarly souped-up bougie outlet – isn't the kind of thing that's valued in foodie circles. Food writers focus on, and even fetishise, the comfort, quiet and calm of the home. There's Nigella Lawson's *How to Be a Domestic Goddess*, which heralded a return to good old-fashioned home cooking, and a new culinary currency under which domesticity (for so long devalued as 'women's work') became the next big thing. Look at the writing of Nigel Slater, and the paeans he writes to the solace of his garden, the joy of seasonality and the cosy virtues of slow, simple home cooking. There's a huge value placed on the feel-good factor of slowing down in an otherwise frantic world: taking time to select the perfect cheese at the farmers' market, or simmering home-made jam on the stove on a dreary day. Because our lives are so hurried, we reach out to slow food to make us whole. But what about tinned tuna fishcakes for families on a budget, getting a job lot of omega acids into the mouths of fussy eaters? Or the ease of throwing some pre-cooked chicken through a pasta sauce for easy, filling protein? Cheapness, simplicity and abundance can coincide with goodness. We often forget within foodie circles that the long way round isn't necessarily the best.

This class-stratified menu isn't a new thing. The gold standard for 'real' food has long traced the dividing line between the accessible and the elite. In Victorian Britain, white bread – uneconomical for the bran and germ it left out – found favour among the wealthy, while the poor ate heavier, healthier brown bread. Today, it's brown bread (especially when aspirationally coded 'whole', 'artisan', 'granary' or 'farmhouse') that signals a loftier kind of eating. White bread is cheap and plentiful, and so its stock has plummeted. When sugar was expensive and alluringly rare in Elizabethan England, it was the wonder of the ruling classes; now highly sugared, processed drinks, sweets and treats are considered the vice of the poor, as the wealthy turn increasingly towards low- or no-sugar diets. A particularly telling divide is the use of 'natural' sugars, adding a microgram of some nutrient or other by using expensive raw honey, where cane sugar could have done more or less the same job at a fraction of the cost. Anyone would think it wasn't about health at all.

Happy shopper

Picture the scene: it is early 2008, and a dark storm is spreading across the country like an inkblot. Frozen McCain potato rostis are sold out across the south of England, and finding an Asda frozen mushroom risotto is nigh impossible. Journalists are ruminating ten to the dozen on the state of cookery today. Restaurant critic Giles Coren generously proclaims in a national newspaper, 'If you can't cook and you can't afford to go out, eat a cheese sandwich' – from the comfort of his well-heeled wined-and-dined London lifestyle. At the heart of the hurricane, sitting regal on her throne as the queen of home cooking is Delia Smith: she has just released her cookbook *Delia's How to Cheat at Cooking*, and she's started something bigger than she knows.

The premise of *Delia's How to Cheat at Cooking* was simple: in the face of an increasingly puritanical food culture, she wanted to provide normal people with 'cheats' to demystify the art of cooking, cut down on food waste and unclutter our kitchens of useless gadgets and gizmos. Tinned mince took the place of fresh stuff, while frozen chargrilled aubergine slices cut out the fuss of slicing, salting and grilling the aubergine yourself. Swimming blithely upstream, Delia was a salmon breaching the stagnant waters of the home cooking fantasy. Rather than clawing at some hazy dream of a from-scratch kitchen of domestic bliss, she looked at the limitations of ordinary kitchens and the time constraints we're bound by in our busy lives, and made a concession to the anxieties that so many of us have about cooking a whole meal from nothing. While other cooks were telling us how to confit a duck or jar our own jams, Delia was saying, as clear as day: it's OK for cooking to be easy.

Not all of the recipes in the book were particularly appetising, and some even lengthened the journey to a good meal by relying on ingredients that, while designed to cut corners, could only be found in a select few shops. What's more, the Delia phenomenon meant that these ingredients were before long sold out in even those limited stores where they'd once been stocked. Some were disappointed by the environmental impact of relying on pre-packaged, frozen and tinned ingredients, while others just bemoaned the death of kitchen creativity, as though throwing a tin of fried onions in an omelette would stifle the hearts and minds of a nation.

But I like the book. I like this rare acknowledgement that we don't all have the time, resources, skills, confidence, energy, ability or money to cook from scratch every day. If you want to make a moussaka with cheese sauce out of a bottle, because it won't go off in the cupboard, and it's easy, and the kids like it, then so what? Even in a country as wealthy as Britain, there remain urban 'food deserts', where fresh foods are difficult to access. In deprived areas, accessible shops are often small supermarkets or convenience stores, and the selection of fresh fruit, veg, meat and fish in these shops can be exceptionally poor. Without taking a bus ride or paying extra for a home delivery from a larger supermarket, people in these areas may have to fall back on tins and jars, prepared meals and frozen foods. What's more, a 2016 study found that half of all people in poverty in Britain are either disabled or live with a disabled person. The effects of poverty, disability, mental health, employment, caregiving and isolation are huge when it comes to what we're able to cook, and a cookbook that even inches towards a more compassionate food philosophy is a cookbook that I can support. It takes a particular kind of short-sightedness to – still bleary with bloat from your latest expensed, expensive meal – sit back on your throne and decree that those less fortunate than you should just eat a cheese sandwich and be done with it. It smacks of 'let them eat Hovis'.

Luckily, there's a push towards a more egalitarian food media brewing in books like Jack Monroe's *A Girl Called Jack*, or Caroline Craig and Sophie Missing's *The Cornershop Cookbook*. Well away from the aspiration and lofty dreams of so many food books, these recipes are designed to take us, our budgets, our kitchens and our skills as they are, and from those things cook something wonderful. Below are a few recipes I've developed with this ethos in mind.

Back-to-basics potato curry

This no-fuss, store-cupboard curry sauce is a real hit with kids thanks to its mildness. Potato leaves the sauce velvety smooth, while the carrot adds sweetness that balances the salty depth of the soy sauce. Everything here should either be in your kitchen cupboards already, or available from even the most sparsely stocked convenience store.

Drain two 500–600g tins of potatoes, and a 300g tin of carrot slices. Mash a quarter of the potato with all of the carrot thoroughly with a masher or fork in a bowl – they should already be really soft. Fry a finely chopped large onion in a large saucepan with a tablespoon of vegetable or sunflower oil, until tender and translucent. Add three finely chopped cloves of garlic and fry for a further minute, before adding two tablespoons of honey (or brown sugar), two tablespoons of light soy sauce, 1½ tablespoons of mild curry powder, the potato and carrot mash mixture and 500ml of chicken stock. Stir together until smooth, then simmer for 5–10 minutes, until slightly thickened. Season to taste with salt and pepper. At this point, you can purée the sauce with a hand blender or food processor if you have one, but this is completely optional. Cut the remaining potatoes in half and add to the sauce, and simmer for a further 10 minutes, until heated through. Serve with loads of fluffy rice. Serves four.

No-bake chocolate hazelnut fudge bars

When you live in a flat or house share without a fully equipped kitchen, dessert can be difficult. So many desserts need to be baked in an oven, or stored in a freezer – these fudge bars are a lower maintenance alternative to all that. Stick 200g of bourbon biscuits in a food bag and crush using a rolling pin (or hammer or anything you can bash with), until you have a crumbly powder. Melt 75g of butter, then stir the crumbs into it. Press into the base of a 15×22cm tin (or any container roughly the same size). Put in the fridge to set. Meanwhile, finely chop 100g of dark chocolate and set aside. Pour a 400g tin of condensed milk into a small, heavy-based pan and set over a low heat. Stir constantly, covering the whole of the bottom of the pan with your spoon, because the milk will quickly catch, brown and burn if you don't! As soon as it reaches a simmer, turn off the heat and add 125g of chocolate hazelnut spread, such as Nutella (although supermarket own brands are far cheaper and just as good!). As soon as the chocolatey condensed milk mixture is smooth, stir in the chopped dark chocolate. Pour over the biscuit base, then place in the fridge to set for an hour. When you're ready to eat, cut into little bars. Makes 12–18 bars.

Herby pesto flatbreads

Most breads need special protein-rich flour, yeast, and lots of time – none of which are things that we usually have in the kitchen. These flatbreads are different: using just ordinary flour and baking powder, they take less than 20 minutes from mixing bowl to mouth. Preheat the oven to 180°C/fan 160°C/gas mark 4 and grease two baking trays with plenty of olive oil. Mix 250g of plain flour and two teaspoons of baking powder (or just use 250g of self-raising flour and no baking powder), and stir in two teaspoons of mixed dried herbs and a pinch of salt and pepper. Add two heaped tablespoons of green or red pesto to the flour mixture, then slowly stir in 90–110ml of water. You need just enough water to make the mix come together to a soft and pliable dough, but you don't want it to be sticky. On a lightly floured surface, roll half of the dough out until it's just under half a centimetre thick. Repeat with the other half of the dough, then lay the flatbreads on the trays. Drizzle the tops with more olive oil, sprinkle with dried herbs and a little salt, and arrange 8–10 tomato wedges on the top of each one. Bake for 10 minutes, swapping them over on the shelves halfway through. Cut into big wedges and enjoy as they are, or with a herby dip. Serves four, as a snack.

Supermarket sweep

While I'm on the topic of eating cheaply and practically, I want to talk about supermarkets. Supermarkets are increasingly maligned, and often for good reason. They've been blamed for the gradual boa constrictor squeeze of local shops and markets, and the monopolisation of the British grocery bill. In 2004, Joanna Blythman wrote *SHOPPED* – an investigative book all about the hegemony of a few big supermarket chains, and the tightening control that these companies have over our diets. A huge number of us rely on supermarkets for our food shopping, and by competitively cutting prices, these supermarket giants are making life for producers and farmers harder than ever, and holding their customers captive all the while. But it's not all bad news, and I worry that this view of supermarkets as the devil's own marketplace is oversimplifying what's actually a complicated issue – and one that hits right to the heart of our relationship with food.

Because they're so ubiquitous now, it's easy to take supermarkets, and all the convenience they offer, for granted. They are giants in the fabric of our landscape – as ageless as the cliffs of Dover or the rolling Yorkshire dales. Except they're not. It wasn't until 1950 that the first self-service grocery store opened – a Sainsbury's in Croydon – and revolutionised the way we shop. Until that point, shopping was an all-morning endeavour: a trudge from sales assistant to sales assistant, ordering meat, then bread, then canned goods from each counter in turn as though you were visiting the stations of the cross. But with the introduction of self-service, the foundations were laid for a kind of shopping that was easy, self-guided and – crucially – quick. This was the beginning of the supermarket as we know it today, as shops grew bigger and sleeker, able to handle ever-growing numbers of customers. By 1964, the first out-of-town supermarket had opened. At the time of writing, Sainsbury's, Tesco, Morrisons and

Asda have, between them, nearly 6,000 branches operating across the UK.

Supermarkets are at the heart of grocery shopping in the UK, then – to the extent that many of us (myself included) can barely imagine a life without them. And I, for one, love them. These places are cathedrals: high-ceiling, bathed in light, filled with every imaginable indulgence that mother nature has to offer. The rituals of the supermarket trip – finding the trolley, weaving through aisle upon aisle, bringing with you a token list as a sign of good faith, then swerving hungrily away from the list the second you enter the confectionery section – these things are banal and comforting and, in their own way, wonderful. I love how every supermarket cloaks its shelves in a different kind of regalia. I take pride in being able to tell a Tesco from an Asda simply by the format of the ingredients list on the back of a packet. I've spent a lifetime being nourished by these giants, and whether it's love or resignation, I can't help feeling attached to them.

There's a lot of awfulness about the supermarket, too, obviously. The crowds and the wayward trolley and the unexpected item in the bagging area – these are just the start of it. There's also the trickiness of retailers who, knowing that we're all pressed for time, plant pricier big-brand products at eye level, and tuck own brands and bargain options away in the shelves by our feet. We're pushed towards the false economies of buy-one-get-one-free offers and have our shopping habits carefully monitored by Big Brother in our points card. We're patronised by being presented only with the brightest, roundest fruit and veg (while the ugly ducklings are sent to the compost heap), and too often lured into buying overpriced 'health' foods sold on false promises. And the waste is horrific. In 2014, men were prosecuted for 'stealing' out-of-date food from the bins behind a branch of Iceland.

But still the supermarket has a gravity that's impossible to escape. Of course, there's something special about threading your way through a bi-monthly farmers' market, or cherry-picking the best chicken from the butcher's shop, or perusing the window display of an artisan bakery, but these things aren't everyday pleasures for the majority of us. We need convenience, and good value, and the luxury of variety. Especially given our increasingly diverse population, and our changing tastes, the variety of the supermarket is invaluable. When people call point-blank for us to boycott supermarkets, they seldom spare a thought for how the average person will afford, or find time for, the alternative. Maybe, one day, local businesses will be protected by government, and a little of the power of the big supermarkets will be snatched away, to make a slightly fairer shopping world. I really hope this happens. But until then, the best that any of us can do is to shop to feed ourselves and the people around us, cutting corners when we have to, and taking the long route round if we can. Shop wherever you can to put food on your plate, without breaking the bank. We all need to eat, after all.

Hanging with Rihanna in a bodega

A supermarket aisle, stacked high with rainbow packets shouting at you from every shelf, is a cubist masterpiece. The counter of a chicken shop, festooned with the absolute worst photos of the delicious food on offer, is a postmodern delight. Fast food is an Essex girl: ostentatious, immodest and perfect, upsetting the delicate dispositions of snobs the world over. The royal purple of the Cadbury empire is the new black, or for postmodern chic you could plump for a bold capsule wardrobe in the primary splashes of red, yellow and blue of a tub of Bird's Custard Powder.

Food is fashion. The food choices we make on a daily basis have as much to do with who we are and where we stand in the world as they do about the contents of our stomachs; this is style over substance, and it's fun. There's not a single food choice that can't be pinned on the map of your likes and dislikes, passions and phobias, to create a pop profile of your food fashion clique. Your Nando's order is a star sign, the contents of your fridge is a one-stop personality quiz. Avocado and pineapple are so in vogue right now that you'll just as likely see someone in an avocado t-shirt as in a band tee, while pineapple ornaments are *the* cute millennial house accessory du jour. Like every other pop culture tributary, food swirls into the zeitgeist and shapes the image of an entire generation. Ten years ago, bakeries were saturated with cutesy cupcakes; today, it's all about a more macho world of sourdough, wood-fired this and artisan that. We look back on arctic roll, prawn cocktail and the cabbage soup diet with the same bafflement as we do Nickelback and flares. Someday soon, everything you know and love – kale, chia seeds, gluten-free faddism – will have all the appeal of a power suit and corkscrew perm.

Food fashion is going through a strange phase right now, though. This is the anti-fashion fashion – the equivalent of the 'boho chic' and indie rock of the noughties – a kind of back-to-basics Holden Caulfield 'authenticism' that says: 'I am the real deal in a world of phonies.' It's subdued and self-referential, speaking the language of organicism, sparseness, simplicity and light. Take a look at today's most popular food Instagrams and blogs and this aesthetic plays out in the scrubbed wood tables, elegant stoneware and minimalist vibe. This is the world of *Kinfolk*, a glossy magazine where rich white people return to the 'purity' of natural living, with stripped pine furniture (reinvented Ikea) and wholesome, simple foods (reinvented *cucina povera*). Two thousand and thirteen saw the publication of *The Modern Peasant* – a food book exploring the reclaiming of urban space for growing and producing trendy, decidedly un-peasantlike food. Even

Marie Antoinette wanted a taste of the simple life. This kind of sparse, clean aesthetic is a de facto ruling out of the visual cacophony of supermarkets, big brands and colourful, attention-grabbing fast food slogans. There's no room in this sterilised world for picking up an emptied cardboard box from the shelves of Lidl and filling it with tins of chopped tomatoes and sweetcorn.

The problem is food fashions are in their very essence aspirational. They are rarely just a celebration of the here and now – of the things that make us happy and satisfy our stomachs. More often than not, it's desire that sets the standard, whether that's desire for a more luxurious life, a healthier body or a sleeker aesthetic. Having stuff – clothes, a roof over your head, a mobile phone – is no longer a marker of wealth, and even the very poorest can deck their lives out with feel-good purchases, trinkets and mementos. And so class signifiers have had to evolve beyond just the accumulation of stuff. Enter the cult of Marie Kondo (the popular Japanese lifestyle author who has encouraged us, as a nation, to get organised and clear our lives of excess stuff), bare living environments and light, bright apartments. This is a new kind of consumerism, marked not by the amount of stuff you have, but the amount of nothingness you can afford. The possessions you have need to 'spark joy', the food you have should be pure, perfect and natural. Somehow the whole of capitalism has inverted so that the conditions of good taste now lie in nothingness, nature and blank space. I can't help but think of Dolly Parton's infamous quote: it costs a lot of money to look this cheap.

But there's a startling asymmetry crystallising between the purity fetishism of the food world and the flavour of broader popular culture – music, fashion, art. While wellness was fussing over the state of its cuticles, Rihanna was doing a photoshoot for *Paper* magazine set in a bodega, channelling afrofuturist magic in the chilled aisle, among the canned goods, and behind the till of an everyday corner shop. As long ago as 2003, Kelis stirred sex into the home-style cooking of an all-American diner when she released 'Milkshake', while Beyoncé brought lemonade to the music hall of fame in the title of her 2016 album. Back in the 1960s, Andy Warhol, with his Campbell's soup can prints, got this aesthetic rolling – clashing the hauteur of art gallery walls with loud super-market consumerism. These pop cultural offerings have immortalised the food microcosms they portray: normal, trashy, hedonistic food equals sex, money, cool and encodes a particular kind of 'back to my roots' authenticity. This isn't the rarefied world of fine dining and contrived stardom – this is a delicious taste of pop genius.

Meanwhile, the staid conventionalism of *Bon Appétit* magazine recently found its match in Katy Perry's 'Bon Appétit' videos which shows the singer being prepped, preened and poached ready for eating. In 2014, models took to the Moschino runway in the red and yellow regalia of some alternate reality McDonald's, the golden arches of M for … Moschino emblazoned loudly across their chests. The same year, Chanel took its catwalk to a model supermarket, parading models through aisles of cheap and cheerful foods in thousand-dollar clothes. What's happening here, with all these anomalous meldings of high and low, is a muddling of the founding precept of both fashion and food: the sticky, unwieldy, useless idea that there is any such thing as good taste.

I love this unabashed, uncouth fashion lexicon. I love the upending of the old hierarchies of taste, and I fizz with hope at the thought that maybe the whims of fashion might, for once, work to elevate and celebrate the culture of the many, not the few. But it's impossible not to be sceptical when, ensconced in the world of high fashion, luxury labels use the imagery of 'low' culture for products that are designed for a fashionable elite. People who seldom step foot in McDonald's are wearing the sweater, while Chanel appropriates the aesthetic of an everywoman culture that its customers surely know little about. All the while, the bodies cloaked within these designer clothes are, more often than not, idealised portraits of thinness and conventional femininity. There isn't much room in this tongue-in-cheek junk food fashion for bodies that reflect the real diversity of the fast food restaurant-frequenting public. I can't help but feel that sometimes these symbols of pop food culture are harvested, recycled and co-opted in quite a cynical way. That's not to say that chicken nuggets don't belong in the world of high fashion. But there's a big difference between a normal person seeing the transcendent beauty of a packet of Monster Munch, and a corporation exploiting that image with a kind of cool irony, and for a huge price tag.

From both ends of the pop cultural spectrum, there's a squeezing of food culture, pushing it on the one hand towards aspirational minimalism, and on the other towards irreverent maximalism. I want you to follow the whims of fashion sometimes, because that's fun and silly and gives you a sense of belonging somewhere in this world. If you want an avocado-themed phone case, go for it – just like you'll inevitably go for that lemon yellow jumper that will not, and will never, suit you. But spread yourself across the trends: be part mum-buying-pesto-for-a-weeknight-tea, part bougie bitch with the Moschino tee. Be the Chicken Connoisseur in an age of diet shills, and pick-and-mix the diet of your dreams. Whatever you do, make it fun. There is no such thing as Good Taste – only good tastes.

Speaking in tongues

Social capital can take you to the supermarket, and food trends send your trolley veering towards one aisle or another. Money helps you slide through the checkout, time puts a home-cooked meal on your plate, and an able body can lift a forkful of food from table to lips. But all of this counts for nothing if, at that moment when the food yields to the warmth of your hungry mouth, it doesn't taste good. No matter what nutrition, fashion or fad might dictate about the correct balance of the dinner plate or the state of your greens, the heart of taste lies not in reason or aesthetics or careful consideration, but in the machinations of your tongue, nose and throat. Most of all – and perhaps unexpectedly – taste happens in the dark, damp, strange recesses of the human brain.

Put a square of chocolate in front of you, and look at it. Just look at it with longing eyes and feel your mouth begin to salivate and your tongue slowly, pensively move. Already, your body is limbering up for the magic of the first taste: your brain is sifting through memories of foods you've eaten before, and all the sweet, bitter, fragrant or blissful sensations that came surging with that mouthful. In the case of milk chocolate, you're no doubt remembering the taste of sweet, soothing smooth cocoa, and the mellow warmth of vanilla. (Incidentally, castoreum – a cheaper alternative to vanilla occasionally used in dairy products – is synthesised from the anal glands and castor sacs of beavers! Something to think about.) The body keeps the score, and the rich caloric value of this little square of chocolate will be eagerly anticipated by a gut that craves energy, and a brain that thrives on the familiar thrill of pleasure pathways awakened when we eat, have sex, take drugs.

Now, take the chocolate between your thumb and index finger. Feel its smoothness, waxiness, crispness or heft. Focusing all your attention on the chocolate, bring it towards your nose and breathe deep. This is orthonasal olfaction or, to put it more simply, just the act of smelling through your nose. Roasted cacao beans, which form the backbone of chocolate as we know it, have hundreds of aromas all interwoven in a single sniff, and not all of them are as pleasurably predictable as the toasted and coffee flavours you'd expect: aroma compounds include ones that smell like anything from raw beef to cabbage and human sweat. Concentrate on what notes you can pick out in the chocolate you have in front of you, but don't feel too bad if you can't decipher the finer details: I've been sat here for half an hour with the chocolate under my nose and all I can really say is that it smells like chocolate. Lucky for those of us with unrefined palates, though, our brains are pretty adept at taking all the myriad smells and subtleties that assault our nostrils every day and not dwelling on them too much. Scents get spun together, and we can take a situation, or food, as a whole rather than being able to pick out every individual odour.

It's time to eat the chocolate. Slip it into your mouth and, instead of chewing, just sit it on your tongue, press it against the roof of your mouth and let it slowly melt to a pool of velvet sweetness. Finally, it's time for the tongue to shine. Covered in tiny tastebuds, it is dense with little protein receptors that can detect bitter, sweet and umami (the savoury kick of soy sauce, meat and mushrooms) flavours. It can also pick out saltiness, sour tastes and even – according to some scientists – detect calcium and fat. These little taste detectors cover the surface of the tongue in tiny bumps and, contrary to the received wisdom that you taste sweet on the tip of your tongue, bitterness on another part and so on, we actually detect all tastes on all areas of the tongue. With the chocolate smoothly melting over your tongue, you should be able to taste it in all its glory: slightly bitter, sweet, mellow, rich with vanilla, dark with the familiar cocoa taste.

But funnily enough, the tongue isn't actually particularly good at tasting at all. Pinch your nose, and taste the difference. Without the help of smell – specifically, retronasal olfaction, which means smelling through the back of the mouth and throat – the chocolate tastes flat. You may taste plain sweetness, or bitterness, but all the glistening nuance is gone. You can do something similar by tasting a spoonful of cinnamon sugar with, and then without, the aid of your nose. It's in the nose that we 'taste' the overwhelming majority of flavours that we experience when we put foods in our mouths. This smell sensation, in conjunction with all the sensory overload of the texture of our food, the movement of chewing, the sound of crunching, swilling and sucking, and the warmth or coolness of our mouthful, comes together to paint the vibrant, delicious experience of what it means to taste.

Just how such complex tasting systems came to exist is something that's still contested. Bitter flavours are likely to be unpalatable to us because of the bitterness of several toxic plants, poisons and other natural nasties. Meanwhile, sweetness remains a very human vice because it signals calorie-rich, simple carbohydrates from which our bodies can easily derive energy. What's more, sweetness has been proven to actually reduce pain perception in babies and children, lending some weight to parents plying their kids with lollipops or gummy bears after a nasty fall or a vaccine jab. These preferences and aversions are so strong that even babies born with anencephaly (a severely life-shortening and often fatal condition where infants are born with much of their brain missing, including the 'thinking hub' cortex) smile when given sweet solutions, and grimace in response to bitter ones. These tastes are so innate that they can even hold fast when the only brain to reside in is the most primitive, 'reptile' brain stump. That's some excuse for not eating your sprouts.

But the degree to which we experience these likes and dislikes is far from predetermined. Take bitter tastes, for example. Stories often make the headlines about 'super-tasters' – the 25% of the population who have increased sensitivity to bitterness, making foods like beer, brassicas and coffee particularly unpleasant for them. But what about the rest of us? Somewhere between twenty and forty different genes determine how many bitter receptors we have, and roughly 25% of people have significantly fewer than you'd expect, leaving them happy, in theory, to eat slightly bitter foods. This lack is often framed as a disadvantage – a marker of an indiscriminate poor taste – but it may have its roots in survival. In countries where malaria is common, people often have reduced sensitivity to bitterness. This allowed nomadic populations to eat (and presumably enjoy) certain plants that carried a slightly bitter taste and contained small quantities of cyanide. This cyanide, while negligible enough to pose no threat to the people who ate it, would poison malarial parasites and so help to guard against malarial outbreaks.

The differences in perception of taste are huge between human groups, and even bigger between us and different species. Cats, for example, no longer carry the gene that allows them to experience sweetness. If they're partial to a saucer of milk, then it's not the creamy sweetness they're enjoying. Rats, on the other hand, go crazy for water laced with a starch called maltodextrin – a compound that we humans can't actually taste. And yet even when we can't consciously taste something, that doesn't mean the brain doesn't have its own ways of keeping us safe. With maltodextrin, it was found that sportspeople who washed their mouth with maltodextrin solution (which tasted like water) outperformed those who'd rinsed their mouth with actual H_2O. Despite the fact that they couldn't taste the starch, and didn't ingest it, their bodies seemed to 'know' that there was a difference. By some wizardry, our brains can do all kinds of tasting without us even knowing about it.

This isn't the only trick that our brains play on us when it comes to flavour. The brain – not the tongue or nose or mouth – is the biggest taste organ we have, and much of the tasting it does confounds the reasoning of the rational, conscious, wrinkly 'thinking' brain. Add a few drops of red food dye into white wine, for instance, and even self-avowed foodies can be tricked into thinking they are drinking red wine. We can be swayed towards food cravings by static, tasteless little words – onomatopoeic words like 'crisp' and 'squidgy' on a menu bypassing thoughtful discernment and cutting straight to our senses. And we are masters of the art of kidding ourselves even when it comes to our tastes and fancies. The show *Eat Well for Less* shakes up the expensive shopping and eating habits of a different family each week. As part of their new diet, the family is given a kitchen full of plain-packaged foods, most of which are cheaper alternatives, but some of which are sneaky inclusions of their 'usual brands'. Time after time after time, a participant will sit back, chew thoughtfully and – convinced that they're eating a cheap-and-nasty version of their pricey big brand favourite – declare that they don't like the swap one jot, and that they'd never buy this one given the choice. This is the power of expectation at work. No matter what information our tastebuds and noses are feeding us, we can be delighted or disgusted at the behest of our contrary brains.

This cleverness of our culinary brains goes a long way towards explaining why our tastes are so incredibly diverse. Although some of us are more sensitive to bitterness, or perhaps have genetic predispositions towards liking or disliking certain foods (coriander, to some people with a specific gene, tastes soapy rather than fresh and herbal), we are most of us made of more or less the same stuff – tastebuds that have honed our palates through thousands upon thousands of years of evolutionary trial and error, noses that have grown sensitive to goodness and poison. Why, then, do some people hate Haribo, or crave charcoal? What gene could possibly account for someone not liking mozzarella or loving tripe?

The answer lies not in chemicals or taste receptors or any real measurable scientific vector. We have the tastes we have, for the most part, because of the experiences we have had – a heady mix of memory of disgust and pleasure. Association might mean that we align rice with the comfort of mum's attention, and love it for life. It could also make us think back on the bitterness of a mouldy blueberry we once ate, every time we cross paths with a platter of perfectly ripe, sweet berries. At some point in the latter half of a foetus's development, the little nasal plugs that block the baby's nose begin to dissolve, and amniotic fluid – ripe with the flavours of the food that mum has eaten – floods the baby's mouth, nose and throat. A study has shown that the babies of mothers who drank carrot juice during their third trimester or while breastfeeding were much more receptive to carrot flavours when weaned. We tend to like what we know, and fear what we don't, no matter the paradox of not liking what we've never tasted: our first tentative *in utero* tastes set the blueprint for every flavour we love or loathe for the rest of our lives. In this tangle of personal memory, biology, upbringing and evolution, the idea of an across-the-board standard of good taste means nothing at all. Peanut butter and anchovy sandwiches? Go for it. Chocolate smeared with Marmite? Be my guest. Taste works in mysterious ways.

Bitch, we're eating brioche

I can remember the shimmering joy that ran through me when I first realised that I might be queer. I already knew that my gaze stuck a second too long on other girls, and that I might want to date some of them. I knew how much I loved to be loved by men, but that maybe my husband one day would be a wife. I knew that I could taste sweet perfume or have the sharp punch of aftershave wrap around me, and be just as happy either way. But I didn't know that I could be all of these things at once, be around other people like me, and live my fullest truth. Realising that I could be openly, vulnerably queer was something that only really came to me when I came to terms with food. This is a story about hunger.

Food and sexuality dance on opposite sides of the same mirror. Consume and consummate, eat out and 'eat out', desire, crave, be hungry for and lust after. A hotdog in this fairground mirror skews and swells into a dick; a ripe fruit, cut in cross-section, is crude, vulvic fertility. The language we use is thick and lascivious, sliding between euphemisms and outright expletives as we navigate the double-entendre-rich territory between the hunger of our bellies and the lust of our loins. This duality – food and sex, appetite and desire – even peppers mainstream media: M&S adverts titillating with suggestively cascading spumes of champagne, and shots of chocolate bars slowly sliding into lipsticked mouths. For a while, pumped up on testosterone and coke, celebrity chefs became the new faces of sex, drugs and rock 'n' roll.

And this muddled vocabulary of hunger isn't just seedy innuendo. The language we use to talk about food is gendered through and through. This is what seasons steak with masculine virility, and huffs, puffs and blows down the gleeful effeminacy of a gingerbread house. We have 'girly' and 'manly' foods, 'frilly' and 'no-nonsense' ways of cooking. These ideas, written into our language, designate different foods for different people, and tell us what we really *should* be eating. All of this happens within a heteronormative framework where heterosexuality is the default, which means that any food that diverges from values of that heterosexuality risks being labelled 'gay' in turn. Within this fragile web of contradictions, a bunch of lads can single out one of their own for 'looking gay' for choosing a leaf salad and grilled fish at lunch, but prove their heterosexuality by slapping each other's naked, glistening butts in the rugby club showers.

Not surprisingly, LGBTQ+ people suffer in this sticky web. Bisexuality, for instance, has long been dismissed as a 'greedy' whim, as though bisexual people are stalking the halls of sensible suburban households in the dead of night – stealthy babadooks hungering for your husbands *and* your wives, hoarding them in our dens of queer depravity. By the same token, gay male identities become warped when viewed under the distorting, heteronormative lens of food and sex. The sexuality of queer men is one of excess, debauchery and mindless lust, we are told through countless pointed jabs in film, television and literature. The old order of things dictates that women are makers, while men consume. In its very essence, then, even the sight of two men feeding one another (let alone consuming one another's bodies) is a subversive thing.

Food plays a pivotal role in implying male queerness in Alfred Hitchcock's films. In *Strangers on a Train*, for example – a film ripe with erotic tension between its two male leads – handsome, unsettling, eccentric Bruno orders lamb, French fries and chocolate ice cream for lunch, whereas the more straightforward Guy (soon to be led astray by Bruno's bad influence) plumps for the straighter option of hamburger and coffee. This scene was eventually cut from the American version, but as David Greven explains in *Reel Food: Essays on Food and Film*, the subtext is clear: Bruno embodies a kind of effete, European masculinity that poses a danger to the very fabric of the society he inhabits. He even says to Guy, his words dancing playfully across the queerness implicit in the film: 'I don't think you know what you want.'

In his essay for food website Food52, United States-based

food writer Mayukh Sen describes how his queer and Bengali identities are both marginalised and, through this cultural squeezing, condense into the sweet, heavy form of fruitcake. Although much of the fruitcake we eat here in the UK is viewed as a stolid, reliable, English kind of thing, it actually has roots that run deep into Bengali soil. In West Bengal, Mayukh explains, fruitcake – viewed by the white Americans that he has built his life among as an off-putting oddity – is relished rather than reviled. And running parallel to this narrative is the history of 'fruitcake' as a slur levelled at queer people. Between these two histories sits Mayukh, queer and Bengali, filling his belly with hate he weathers. He has his cake and eats it, too.

In another essay about queerness and food, writer John Birdsall breaks free of the ways that he is cornered, hemmed in and suffocated in the macho world of professional kitchens: 'my *salades composées* were thickets of yearning, drifts of leaves and flowers, sprigs of herbs and tiny carrots that looked like they had been blown there by some mighty force of nature'. This is the subversion of all the received wisdom we have about food and worth. If queerness is excess, let queer food be the most beautiful, luxurious indulgence. If queerness is frilly, let queer cooking be as romantic as Cathy and Heathcliff tumbling dizzily across the moors. If queerness is in bad taste, in the words of Birdsall: *bitch, we're eating brioche.*

Wherever there is the sequestering of LGBTQ+ foods and traditions of eating, there will always be a queer eating a brioche in extravagant protest. Meredith Kurtzman, 'a crusty, West-Village hippy lesbian', pretty much single-handedly inspired New York City's love of gelato. The three pillars of American food writing in the late twentieth century – Richard Olney, Craig Claiborne and James Beard – were all gay. There is a long tradition of queer trailblazers redefining the culinary arts, but the influence of queer people goes well beyond just holding to account the macho world of the professional kitchen.

'Bad taste' bleeds into the very stuff we're made of: queer communities historically aligning themselves with obscenity, kitsch, camp, and tasteless, tactless excess. The queer defence is an inversion: the accusations levelled at us in the name of 'good taste' are glamorised, weaponised and held close to us. It's impossible to talk about these matters of taste without talking about food. If 'poncey' food is over-the-top, too rich, too fancy, the only thing to do is recline on a chaise longue surrounded by pastel pink macaroons in some Marie Antoinette fantasy. If the prevailing food fashion is for tasteful minimalism, we have to build our bodies with baked alaska, lobster thermidor and choux pastry swans with chantilly cream.

'Food has always played an important part in life's rituals,' says the narrator in 1975 cult classic *The Rocky Horror Picture Show*. 'The breaking of the bread, the last meal of a condemned man, and now this meal.' Sat around a table heavy with the staid, traditional regalia of a family roast dinner, a motley crew of misfits and monsters assembles. Among them, standing out like a sore thumb among the strange queer cast, is a Dr Everett Scott, there searching for his missing nephew – a delivery boy. The queer antiheroes are playing it straight, trying hard to put on a facade of normality in front of their distinguished guest, and for the occasion they have rolled out a huge joint of meat, silver platters, and a regiment of knives and forks at every table setting. And yet the whole charade is rudely blown apart when, halfway through the meal, the villainous 'sweet transvestite' Dr Frank N. Furter whisks the tablecloth away to reveal that the whole feast rested on the coffin of a missing delivery boy. Even this most all-American setup is fit to be queered, as our eyes drift from the mutilated corpse to the big joint of roast meat, and from the silverware to Frank's silky stockings. This is the opposite of assimilation into a predominantly straight world – it's the act of making ourselves bigger, badder and queerer, whether that's in the bodies we love or the food we eat.

All this talk of queer food might feel conceptual, but there's a real and urgent hunger that drives this whole machine. Consider the fact that, according to a 2016 study conducted by the Williams Institute, one in four LGBTQ+ adults in the United States couldn't always afford the food that they needed to feed themselves and their family, compared with a figure of one in six for heterosexual people. And what of the research that suggests that factions of the queer community experience disproportionate levels of disordered eating compared with the wider population? There's as much need now as ever for a queer menu – one that puts queer appetites right at the centre of the table, and lines the pockets, wallets and bellies of queer people. This menu would be bright and bold and as diverse as the people who feast on it. It would revel in the marvels of bad taste and upend every hackneyed old food 'do' and 'don't'. Most of all, it would shimmer with the promise of pure pleasure – the total, uninhibited, visceral, 'sinful' pleasure that locks queer love and queer food together in dreadful debauchery. In the words of Dr Frank N. Furter himself:

Give yourself over to absolute pleasure
Swim the warm waters of sins of the flesh

A good egg

God and chocolate

I didn't expect that I would be starting a chapter about food ethics with the royal purple wrapper of a bar of Dairy Milk. Good food – that is, ethical food – we are told, is about the local, artisanal, speciality and handmade. It is chickens slowly fattened, from egg to portly hen, and allowed to roam free in verdant fields. What it isn't is a thick chunk of Crunchie with honeycomb that sets hard in the ripples and rifts of your molars, or a weighty slab of Fruit & Nut, or a finger of Fudge melting sweetly across your gums. But for all the frivolity and lightness that chocolate supposedly symbolises, there are a lot of big issues – questions of faith, morality and goodness – swirled through the Cadbury empire's long history. Somehow, from its privileged position front and centre of supermarket shelves up and down the country, this culinary icon still manages to tell a story about ethics that belies its capitalist credentials. It's a tale that starts a long way from the big bucks of present-day parent company Mondelēz International, in the mid-1800s, in Birmingham.

Chocolate as we know it didn't even exist when Cadbury started trading in 1824. At the time, chocolate meant drinking chocolate, although it was a far cry from the ancient central American *chocolatl* that had inspired the Spanish conquistadors, who had, in turn, brought a taste for chocolate to Europe. Chocolate was in fact so little known in the seventeenth and eighteenth centuries that English and Dutch sailors once threw the precious cargo on a Spanish ship overboard, thinking the cocoa beans were sheep's droppings. The delicacy soon gained traction, however, and in the upmarket chocolate houses of London, the rich, bitter, spiced chocolate drink that the Mayans had enjoyed was modified to fit British tastes, sweetened with a hefty dose of sugar and enriched with milk.

The trouble with some of the early incarnations of this drinking chocolate, however, was their oiliness – a result of the simple grinding down of the whole cacao nib to create thick cocoa 'liquor' that formed the base for these drinks. This paste contained not just the dark cocoa solids that gave chocolate its essence, but also fatty cocoa butter which gave an oily sheen to the chocolate drink. Slowly, producers found a way to separate the solids from the butter, creating cocoa powder from the former. And it was this refinement in drinking chocolate that led, in a roundabout way, to the creation of the solid bar of chocolate we know and love. It was a Bristol-based manufacturer called J. S. Fry & Sons who perfected the chocolate bar by mixing in more of the very cocoa butter that cocoa manufacturers had learned to take out. This cocoa butter combined with the solids, plus a little sugar, made a chocolate that was solid at room temperature. Two years later, in 1849, the Cadbury company followed suit with their own chocolate bar.

It's at this point that something strange begins to brew in the deep cauldrons and rising chimneys of the chocolate factories. John Fry, of J. S. Fry & Sons, was a Quaker. So were the Cadbury boys, George and Richard, and their father John, who had started the company. (Confectionery manufacturer Rowntree's of York, established around the same time, was also the product of a Quaker family.) These were faithful men, members of a religious community that believed in values such as modesty, equality, pacifism and temperance. From a place of spirituality and restraint, how did these few families set in motion the wheels of a national appetite for sweet excess?

Right now, with all the foods of the world available to us at a click or with the most perfunctory sweep of a supermarket shelf, we have cultivated a sense of virtue around minimalism. The whole mood of 'ethical' food is one of self-control, slowness, mindfulness and an almost monastic asceticism. Less is more, and mass-produced chocolate is a decadent, saccharine, symbol for everything this 'moral' food movement rails against. But in the mid-nineteenth century, chocolate hadn't yet assumed this mantle as the foodie bogeyman. In fact, with the temperance movement in full swing, and many religious communities mobilising against what they perceived to be the corrupting power of alcohol in Britain, chocolate became a saviour. Along with tea and coffee, whose stimulant properties were considered a safer alternative to the sinful grogginess of booze, chocolate was a nourishing, sensible drink. And among the ranks of the Quakers, excluded from the best universities and persecuted on the grounds of faith, chocolate represented not just a social force for good, but a business opportunity that could keep their communities afloat.

This ethos carried through to the factories that the Quakers built and the communities that sprung up around them. Bournville, the model village created just outside of Birmingham under the watchful eye of the Cadbury brothers, became a living, thriving emblem of this person-centred approach to business. The goal was to 'alleviate the evils of modern, more cramped, living conditions', and it worked: Bournville thrived, workers felt valued and the company implemented working conditions that wouldn't be written into law for many years to come. It was an anomalous leap forward in the bleak, smog-drenched landscape of the Industrial Revolution. This Quaker business ethic was so respected that it even inspired the kindly-looking white-haired, be-hatted 'Quaker' man on the packets of the famous Quaker Oats – from a company which, despite having no ties to the faith, saw the value of the Quakers' ethical, trustworthy image.

Since then, the promise of the Cadbury vision has soured. A merger with Schweppes in the 1960s finally severed the company's ties to its Quaker roots, and over recent decades it has rolled from strategy to strategy, accruing fiscal mass with every move. The most contentious change to the brand came in 2010 when Mondelēz International (then trading as Kraft Foods) acquired the company and turned its historic Britishness on its head, losing UK jobs in favour of Polish production plants, and making divisive changes to the brand's familiar roster of products: chocolate bars got smaller, Creme Eggs changed their shells and Cadbury's Fairtrade credentials were cast aside in favour of a much-criticised in-house code of ethical trading. Even ethical chocolatiers Green & Black's slipped, launching their first ever non-organic chocolate range after being bought by Cadbury in 2005. The chocolate industry has been under more scrutiny than ever for its complicity in child labour and enslavement under West African suppliers, and yet Mondelēz CEO Irene Rosenfeld received a 31.5% pay rise (taking her compensation to roughly £18.9 million) in 2013.

In a velvety square of Dairy Milk, in a bar of cheap chocolate, in a smart purple wrapper, is written a whole century of food ethics, from small business, to compassionate trading, to corporate boom. Everything that is good and bad, hopeful and cynical, compassionate and cruel comes together in the sweeping cursive of one big name: Cadbury is a case study in the sweetness of a fall from grace. If you thought you could just chill out with your Flake and switch off from the world, think again: that perfect sugar stick is a part of a saga that stretches from heaven to hell and back. From a Charlie Bucket to a Veruca Salt, Cadbury – sweet, moral, Quaker chocolate salvation – is a good nut gone bad.

Forbidden fruit

The trouble with food is, no matter how much we wish it could sit tight in the realm of mindless escapism, it will always contain these muddled, moral multitudes. So much for burying our heads in a Wetherspoon's curry or finding solace from all the ills of the world with a mug of Horlicks: at every step, with every chew, our food is heavy with ethical dilemmas. There are questions of animal welfare and workers' rights, quandaries about sustainability and environmental impact, debates on cultural sovereignty, and concerns over public health. Right now, there's a huge amount of interest in local and seasonal produce, and a distrust of big market forces like supermarkets and multinationals. Ten years ago, people agonised over genetically modified foods and battery eggs. This ethical turmoil throws us in so many directions that the simple question of what's for dinner tonight becomes a social and political minefield.

And not all questions of food and morality sit outside of the fabric of the food itself. Sometimes, regardless of where or how it was made, who suffered and who profited, food carries within it a moral weight that belies the conditions of its existence. It just *is* (or at least, it *seems*) to be good, bad, corrupting, purifying, forbidden, holy or crass: chocolate has a moral character that aligns it with sinfulness and lust; water on the other hand is a cleansing thing, whether it came from a tap in Cleethorpes or a San Pellegrino bottle. Food in and of itself is a tangled symbol of morality.

There is an uneasy rhythm in the beat of our desirous,

hungry hearts. We have lustful bodies that cry out for foods that give them pleasure, and yet we have, at the same time, a guilt that clots in our veins. It's this weird, nervous, syncopated hunger that drives a wedge between want and need, desire and contentment, and has paved the way for just about every food-related neurosis we collectively experience. This trauma goes back way further than Cadbury or conquistadors or even the first cooked meal. It has its roots deep in the virgin soils of Eden and, as with so many things, the blame has fallen squarely at the feet of one unwitting, hungry woman.

'And when the woman saw that the tree was good for food, and that it was pleasant to the eyes, and a tree to be desired to make one wise, she took of the fruit thereof, and did eat' (Genesis 3:7). And so begins the biblical descent into sin via Eve and her big mouth. Every time I read this account of a normal woman frantically rationalising her own 'sinful' appetite, I think of Bridget Jones, and I remember that we've been diligently following in Eve's footsteps ever since.

In Eden, there was value in nothingness and nudity. Food was plentiful and simple, and Adam and Eve could enjoy as much wholesome, vegetarian, unadulterated goodness as they pleased. There was no cooking, and no real way to overindulge or succumb to earthly pleasures unless they gave in, as they eventually did, to the temptation of the forbidden fruit. In this era of plenty, it seems strange that something as innocuous as a piece of fruit could bring the whole of divinity crashing down around it, but switch the wisdom-giving apple to a bar of Galaxy and, perversely, the concept still reigns supreme today. This one little misstep laid the foundations for an entire strand of food thinking that has persevered from antiquity through to now: the crucial, ground-breaking idea that the wants of our bodies stand at odds with the goodness of our souls.

This puritanical equation of food (and by extension, pleasure) laid the groundwork for many centuries of outrage at the decadence and moral decline of societies. For some, gluttony is a mortal sin, while in Ancient Greece, Plato's division of our souls into logical, spirited and appetitive parts put hunger at odds with a sound mind. Hippocrates, the father of medicine and the namesake of doctors' Hippocratic oath, thought that we ought to use our powers of reasoning to temper and guide our wayward, often greedy, natures. The disdain for food and pleasure even picked a path through the spirited Romantic period. In *Jane Eyre*, cruel schoolmaster Mr Brocklehurst describes the inherent corruption in bodily things: 'Oh, madam, when you put bread and cheese, instead of burnt porridge, into these children's mouths, you may indeed feed their vile bodies, but you little think how you starve their immortal souls.'

The uptight Victorians are a crystal-clear case study in this kind of food prudishness. It was the time of the temperance movement (which, as we've seen already, paradoxically gave birth to the UK chocolate market) and a growing sense among religious circles that something ought to be done to curb society's descent into industrialisation and all the ills of city life. Concurrently, across the Atlantic, Reverend Sylvester Graham was hard at work preaching the dangers of meat-eating (he wanted a return to an Eden-era vegetarianism) and begging Americans to prioritise good honest pleasures like family life and plain food. In *A Treatise on Bread and Bread-making*, he wrote that 'there is a far more intimate relation between the quality of the bread and the moral character of the family, than is commonly supposed'. He even invented Graham crackers as a simple, nutritious food that would mitigate against the sinful lures of richer foods. Little did he know that those Graham crackers would, after his death, be reborn as sweet, industrially produced, pleasurable things, and the Graham name would come to stand for sugar-sweet, uninhibited hunger. I think about Graham and his bigotry every time I sit at the breakfast table for a bowl of sickly Golden Grahams, and I smile.

And yet there's another stance on food and morality that's very different from this joy-phobic, buttoned-up, post-Eden nervousness. While some were fretting about the supposed greediness of gastronomy, others saw it as a path to godliness. Rather than food pulling us away from our purest selves and down into the bowels of hell, it was something that – if respected, enjoyed, manipulated – could fill us with a bit of something divine. There's something of this attitude in the New Testament, when Matthew quotes Jesus explaining:

> What goes into someone's mouth does not defile them, but what comes out of their mouth, that is what defiles them … Don't you see that whatever enters the mouth goes into the stomach and then out of the body? … For out of the heart come evil thoughts – murder, adultery, sexual immorality, theft, false testimony, slander. These are what defile a person.
>
> Matthew 15:11–18

At roughly the same time, many miles away in northern India, the high-caste Brahmins shouldered not just a practical, but a moral, religious duty to cook. By shaping the materials that God has given us, we become whole. We were given all this earthly bounty for a reason, and to spurn that splendour would be its own sin. This kind of thinking permeates the belief systems of many people and places, but there's also a class element at play in this moral hierarchy. According to these kinds of food philosophies, there's a big difference between 'barbarians' – eating hunks of raw meat, scavenging, and eating foods straight from the guts of nature – and the ruling classes – chowing down on steak tartare, foraging for wild mushrooms, and eating natural 'whole' foods. There is, of course, no substantive difference between the noble and the savage, but that's no issue. The heart of it is that genteel, considered and aesthetically minded equate with 'good', and necessary and ravenous mean 'bad'. In this view of things, the moral character seems to be as much about who's eating as it is about the food itself.

These two warring ideologies play out to this very day, often even next to one another at the dinner table, or adjacent on the plate. We have a societally enforced gourmandism that tugs us towards gastronomy and food tourism and taste, and a compulsory guilt that tugs in the opposite direction towards purity and restraint. This is the duality of our food culture: we're more open and adventurous than ever before, and also more anxious. The minimalism of 'clean' eating and the diet shills coexist with the maximalism of back-to-back food programming, adverts and books. We can still see the influence of Sylvester Graham in movements like the Real Bread Campaign (understandably, if a little overzealously, trying to pull us away from supermarket loaves and back towards the wholesome goodness of 'real' bread). Food writer and campaigner Michael Pollan stands proud in the pulpit giving dictates on food and morality for a new age, while anti-hero and chef Anthony Bourdain rages from the infernal fires of the professional kitchen. It's no wonder we're confused.

Animal, vegetable, mineral

There is a food chain, and, whether we like it or not, we fit in it somewhere. It doesn't exist on paper or in the minds of scientists, in labs or on blackboards: it is something that we inhabit every single day. It's easy to forget this when we're cradled so tight in the insulating societies around us. But there is a food chain, one that plants us in a field, toes sinking in mud and shit, eyeing up a cow that ate some grass that gave a home to a nest of busy black ants – one of them is weaving up your leg right now. There is another food chain where saltwater stings your skin and the current holds you fast, swimming on the spot. In front of you is a flash of fish, a body like a bullet, and it hurtles straight into your hungry mouth. Some other place, roles are reversed and you feel your body slipping away, piece by piece. A hundred happy maggots make away with your heart.

These food webs are heaven and hell. We like nature when it comes at us in a scarlet-streaked sunset in Tenerife – not when it's all gaping mouths, claws, pincers and bellies. We like to think of ourselves as discerning and rational, and as such we shy away from conversations about where we fit among the violence of the food chain. This makes eating meat particularly conflicting for us, and more people than ever are turning to veganism – an increase of 360% in the last decade – to absolve them of the burden of these tricky decisions. With roughly half a million people in the UK now describing themselves as vegan, the landscape of the UK food market has turned on its head.

As veganism has gained traction, the ethical basis for this diet has become increasingly estranged from the lifestyle it has spawned. It has become blurred with 'clean' eating, and for many has health as its primary incentive. The ethical dimension has become secondary to its supposed wellness-boosting credentials. I fully believe that a vegan diet is just as capable of nourishing a perfectly healthy and happy human as an omnivorous diet – there's room for excess, neglect, imbalance and malnourishment in any diet if we're not careful, and that's no more true of veganism than it is of any other lifestyle. But this superstitious belief in healing and purity through restraint leaves me nervous: it feels like the religious vegetarianism of Victorian pioneers like William Metcalfe and the aforementioned Sylvester Graham – men whose insistence on a meat-free diet came not from real compassion but from a judgemental belief in the loathsome appetites of humans. This way of thinking about vegetarianism and veganism leaves them vulnerable to becoming faddy detoxes and diets, impoverished episodes in our culinary history where we delighted more in control than caring.

I was nervous at first to even tackle the subject of vegetarianism and veganism. These subjects are polarising, and conversations rapidly curdle into diatribes from those who believe in the immorality of animal-based foods in all circumstances, and those who cling onto unbridled meat-eating as though it was a fundamental right. Somewhere flickering in the middle of this fracas is a delicate light of truth. I personally think that the ethos of veganism is commendable – industrial farming practices are indisputably cruel, and if we can't reform that system, it's a good thing to avoid the products it gives us. I also think it's indisputable that veganism is better for the environment. But I'm not a vegan, and I'm fine with that. My year-long foray into veganism worsened an existing eating disorder, and I'm not going to open that Pandora's box again until I'm mentally well enough to deal with it. For a lot of people, dietary rules – no matter how virtuous their motives – can easily descend into obsessive control and even eating disorders. Those with orthorexia take the seemingly innocuous guidelines of this or that diet, and by following them with compulsive rigour, become ill. With that in mind, vegetarian and vegan diets won't always be a viable option for an individual. We each need to find a path that aligns with our morals, while also allowing us to stay happy, healthy and well connected.

The ethical debates that draw the line between 'good' and 'bad' foods are sprawling and contentious: parents shopping for a whole family on a budget might rejoice in the plummeted grocery costs and glistening convenience of big supermarket chains; a weary independent butcher might feel differently. Veganism might be a good and viable option for a twenty-something in the city, but an older couple in the countryside might have to draw the line at vegetarianism if they're to keep up their strength in a community that doesn't yet cater to vegan tastes. A person whose entire family comes together over jollof and chicken on a Sunday might have to hold onto poultry in their diet so as not to lose their anchor in the world. A person with two jobs might rely on the easy comfort of a Greggs Steak Bake to push them through the long working day.

These issues shapeshift depending on where you stand and where your moral compass settles, and more often than not the polarising black and white arguments of revolutionaries and reactionaries break down when pinned against the shimmering, swaying nuance of real life. There is no such thing as a single right way to eat. What's right and moral for one person will be untenable for another, and morality extends way beyond just abstracted conversations about animal sentience or environmental sustainability. Sometimes the only thing we can do is to keep afloat in line with the time-old practices and dictates of the flawed world we live in. With all this in mind, I'm reluctant to join the chorus of prescriptive voices telling you what you should or shouldn't eat. I want to trust in your goodness and your heart and in your desire to give as much to the world as you can, within your financial means and in line with the demands of your busy life.

For the most part, we are kind – we want to do good in the world, and help old ladies across the street, and avoid being cruel, callous or cold. There's a nugget deep within us that carries the remnants of our origins as social, cooperative mammals, and this little mammalian brain makes us gravitate more towards goodness than ill. We often *do* want to buy the kinder coffee, or send our money towards sustainable producers, or whatever it is that we think will be helpful in this contested earth we live in. We want to try to minimise the pain we cause to animals, but we are also selfish, myopic, hungry animals ourselves, and that can make our principles sit uncertainly against our appetites. All of this is OK.

Here are three meal ideas – one with meat, one vegetarian, and one vegan – so that you can make something that tastes good and feeds your body and mind, whatever kind of eater you are.

Nepalese-style chicken dumplings in chilli tomato broth

These dumplings make a little chicken go a long way. You can buy ready-made dumpling wrappers in the freezer section of East Asian supermarkets, so use those if you're not up for making the dough: just defrost them and keep them moist under a damp tea towel as you work. If you do want to make the dough from scratch, here's how it's done: combine 250g of plain flour and a generous pinch of salt in a large bowl, then slowly add 135–150ml of boiling water, combining until the dough is smooth but not sticky. Let it cool for a couple of minutes, then, working carefully to avoid burning your hands, knead the dough for 5 minutes until smooth and elastic. Wrap in cling film and leave to rest while you prepare the filling and soup.

Toast three tablespoons of sesame seeds, two teaspoons of cumin seeds and one teaspoon of black mustard seeds in a dry frying pan for just a minute or so, until the mustard seeds start to pop. Put the seed mix in a grinder along with three-quarters of a teaspoon of ground cinnamon and half to a whole teaspoon of dried chilli flakes. Pulse until finely ground and set aside. Crush four cloves of garlic into a small bowl, finely grate in an 8cm piece of ginger and stir together. In a medium saucepan, heat two tablespoons of oil and fry half of the garlic and ginger mixture until fragrant, then add three-quarters of the ground seed/spice mix. (The remaining garlic/ginger mix and seed/spice mix are for inside the dumplings.) Add 200g of chopped tomatoes, two teaspoons of lemon juice, two teaspoons of caster sugar, half a teaspoon of turmeric and 750ml of boiling water to the pan. Season to taste, then leave to simmer over a low heat.

Roughly chop 50g of red or white cabbage, a handful of fresh coriander leaves and three spring onions, then add to a food processor along with 250g of skinless and boneless chicken thighs (or 250g of chicken or turkey mince). Blitz until everything is well combined and the chicken is sticky. Add the reserved garlic/ginger mix and the seed/spice mix, and blitz once more. Now it's time to make the dumplings.

Cut the rested dough into three chunks (small batches make it easier to work with) and, one by one, roll the pieces out on a floured surface. Roll to around 1mm thick, and almost translucent, then stamp out 10–11cm circles using a pastry cutter. No need to keep the offcuts. Lay the pastry circles out on a plate and cover with a damp cloth to stop them drying out. To assemble, put a teaspoon of the chicken mixture in the middle of each circle, very slightly dampen the edges, and either fold over to a crimped half-moon shape, or gather up all the way around into a little purse shape. Make sure the filling is well sealed in.

Line a steamer rack with circles of greaseproof paper, piercing it with little holes to help the steam filter through. Arrange the dumplings in the steamer (don't crowd them – you'll need to work in a couple of batches), and cook for 12–15 minutes. Check the thickness of the soup, and either reduce it or add a little more water. Ladle the soup into bowls, and place five or six dumplings in each one. Serves four.

Roasted aubergine, feta and lemon fusilli

This is one of those recipes that take pretty much 30 minutes from start to finish and – once you have it in your arsenal – you'll never stop making. Preheat the oven to 180°C/fan 160°C/gas mark 4. Slice a large aubergine into ½cm rounds, and cut a red pepper into very thin long strips. Toss the aubergine, pepper, two whole unpeeled garlic cloves, 75ml of olive oil and plenty of salt and pepper together in a large roasting dish, and bake for 25 minutes. Towards the end of that time, boil 200g of fusilli pasta according to the instructions on the packet. Very finely slice a handful of basil leaves into crinkled little ribbons, and crumble 100g of feta cheese. Once the veg is ready, pluck out the garlic cloves and squeeze the now soft, sweet, fragrant pulp from the skin and into a little dish. Whisk the garlic together with the juice of half a lemon. Gently stir the veg, feta, basil and garlic-lemon dressing through the drained pasta, check the seasoning and serve straight away. This also makes a great cold pasta salad – just hold off mixing everything together until the last minute. Serves two.

Spiced sweet potato stew with hazelnuts

Ground hazelnut creates creaminess without the need for milk or eggs, and adds body and a nutty, savoury kick to this simple stew. Peel three or four large sweet potatoes (you'll need roughly 1kg in total) and cut into 2cm dice. Prepare the spice mix: mix two teaspoons of sweet paprika, half a teaspoon each of cinnamon and ground coriander, and a quarter of a teaspoon each of chilli powder, ground allspice (or ground cloves), nutmeg, ground ginger and coarsely ground black pepper. Now, blitz 100g of hazelnuts to a fine powder in a coffee grinder or food processor (you can also buy ready-ground hazelnuts in some supermarkets). Heat two tablespoons of vegetable oil in a large pan and add four crushed garlic cloves. As soon as the garlic is fragrant, add the spice mix along with three-quarters of the ground hazelnuts, one tablespoon of tomato purée, two teaspoons of lemon juice and a teaspoon of soft light brown sugar. Sizzle for a minute or so, then add the sweet potato and 500–800ml of vegetable stock – enough to just cover the potato. Stir to combine, then bring to a simmer over a medium–low heat. Add a little more stock if needed to cover the sweet potatoes, then cook with the lid on, stirring occasionally, for 20–30 minutes or so. It's ready when the potato is tender and just beginning to break apart at the edges. To serve, cook plenty of fluffy rice, ladle over the stew and sprinkle liberally with the remaining ground hazelnuts. Serves four.

Taboo

Why don't we eat our dead pets? There are lots of things that make sense about cooking the family cat once its happy, pampered life has drawn to a natural close. We would be saved the expense and energy of disposing of the remains, and have an organic opportunity to all come together over its precious little body and appreciate it one last time. It would give people a way to squeeze precious calories and protein from a world where food resources are often scarce, and the joy of having loved and nurtured that meal en route. We would know that we were taking a stand against our society's endemic wastefulness. Most of all, it would be a way to honour the animal: what could be more poignant or respectful than taking the flesh of a treasured thing and making it your own? To eat something is to want to be made of it, and your pet sure as hell wouldn't mind.

But these logical arguments don't really grip when we're talking about something as emotive as pets and the love that we share with them. Reasoning slips and slides across the boundaries of common sense, and we recoil at the coldness of pursuing pure pragmatism in cases where so much heart is involved. In fact, for most of us, the thought of eating our pets – even if that pet has lived a long and happy life, and died peacefully of natural causes – is not just unpalatable, but revolting. We're disgusted at the thought of turning Felix into meatballs or laying the bronzed, crispy carcass of Rover on the kitchen table. And this is OK, because our feelings are important. There will always be some philosophy bro who thinks we should all disregard the cultures and inherited moral compasses we were born into, and just pursue the utilitarian path towards maximum efficiency. I've suffered through enough undergrad philosophy tutorials to know this, because I once *was* that dude. But feelings aren't rational, and can never be. There are certain things that, no matter how much they don't make sense, will always be taboo.

Just why we feel this way about certain things isn't always clear. With the case of pets, it could be that we're repulsed by the idea of eating something with which we have such a close relationship, but then what does that say about farmers who know their cows or sheep or chickens by name, and still happily send them to slaughter? Maybe it's the intelligence of cats and dogs, and the fact that tricks help to humanise them in a way that makes their flesh feel just like ours. But that doesn't align with the fact that pigs – smarter than even dogs – are the most widely consumed animals on the planet, despite being prohibited foods for two of the world's three major religions. We saw first-hand the wheels of the taboo machine in action when several years ago it emerged that consumers had been duped, with horsemeat bulking out 'beef' products on supermarket shelves. The furore that erupted when this happened wasn't just the righteous pursuit of consumer rights, but a furious reaction to the very idea of eating horses at all – fairly advertised or otherwise.

The 1904 St. Louis World's Fair was the largest and most spectacular exhibition the United States, and indeed the world, had ever seen. For a full seven months the fair ran a semi-permanent host of exhibitions, attractions and displays, with contributors from countries around the world and forty-three US states. Drawing over 19 million visitors in total, it was immortalised in *Meet Me in St. Louis* some forty years later. But for all the grandeur of this record-breaking fair, all the novelty and the sprawling curation of the entire globe across a 4.9-square kilometre plot, there was one issue on everyone's lips: the Filipino exhibit, and some people who had eaten dogs.

'About the time the World's Fair city is waking at early morning, one hundred bare-limbed Igorot often sacrifice and eat a dog on the Philippine Reservation ... The Igorot represent the wildest race of savages.' This extract from the fair brochure says in under fifty words what the entire 'Philippine Exhibit' – a massive 47-acre plot of 'villages' populated by over 1,000 Filipino people – was designed to convey. These people, the fair is suggesting in no uncertain terms, are barbarians. The exhibit set out the lives of these many different Filipino ethnic groups like funfair attractions, ready to be gawped at by the millions of people who visited the site during the fair's duration. In a particularly calculated move, the exhibit's organisers even juxtaposed the 'savagery' of the dog-eating Igorot people with the polite conformism of a troop of Filipino soldiers in blue United States army regalia.

This was horror versus humanity, taboo in contrast with tradition. The aim was to engender support for the United States' annexation of the Philippines by showing that Filipino people needed the civilising powers of the Western superpower. As Bel S. Castro explained in an essay for the Oxford Symposium on Food and Cookery, 'the 1904 World's Fair stands apart as a unique situation in history where food, disgust, identity, and power collided ... A ritual of eating and dining became a tool for vilification and was instrumental in pushing forward a political agenda.'

It's baffling to think that the simple practice of eating dog meat was enough to drum up domestic support for the bloody America–Philippines war, but that's just what happened. Food stood for animality, supremacy, conquest and community, and by outraging the sensibilities of dog-loving Americans, the participants of the Philippine exhibit unwittingly stoked the fires of the anti-Filipino propaganda machine. You're allowed to have dogs around your home, in your bed, on your lap and even carrying wedding rings down the aisle, but god forbid you put them on the table.

It is mainly Christian value systems that have moulded our moral codes in the UK, but in other places and under other belief systems, very different food dos and don'ts have taken root. In some Indian states, influenced by the sanctity of cows in Hinduism, the slaughter of cows is not just taboo but illegal. Kosher laws define what foods are acceptable in Judaism, curbing appetites for non-Kosher foods such as pork or shellfish, and placing prohibitions on, for example, eating dairy with meat, as to do so would be to 'cook a young goat in its mother's milk' (Exodus 23:19). In certain tribes in West Malaysia, the taboo status of food depends not just upon the food but also the eater: different people have a different permitted roster of foods to choose from, based on the strength of their spirit. Children might only be allowed small birds, toads and water snails while they build up enough maturity to handle the spirits of larger animals such as deer.

The origin of these dietary commandments isn't always religious, and more often than not they sit at the confluence of culture, common sense, survival and sentiment. In parts of mid-west Nigeria, children are not fed coconut milk for fear that it will make them unintelligent, a belief that has no more base in fact than the belief among American and European parents that a gluten-free diet can alleviate the symptoms of autism. It makes sense that alcohol is so often forbidden considering its poisonous, mind-clouding properties, too. At a certain age, hangovers become so outright vile that I'm tempted to label alcohol unholy myself on occasion. Even when a taboo is written into scripture, there can still be other narratives that run alongside the heaven-sent dictates of good and bad. In the case of pork, it is prohibited under both Islam and Judaism. And yet a contrasting utilitarian account can be written, too. At a time when the fight for food and resources was tough, pigs and humans – both historically scavenging, omnivorous animals – may have competed for resources. Eating pork at that time would have meant making dinner from the competition, and killing two birds (or pigs) with one stone. In a similar way, the British fear of horsemeat could be a manifestation of our one-time reliance on the animals for nobler purposes such as transport and farming. A horse is a lot less useful in the belly than at the plough.

What all of this adds up to is a fuzzy patchwork of rules that twist and skew from place to place. Except for maybe the prohibition on eating human flesh (and even this isn't always enforced), there is no real overarching moral framework that sets the standards for food for all of us. This lack of black and white can be difficult to swallow, and it leads us to sensationalise foods that sit outside of our comfort zone. We build dividing walls in our minds between 'us' – good, righteous, kind – and 'them' – dog-eaters. We barricade ourselves into our kitchens and hold our cats and dogs tight to our chests. 'This is normality!' we cry in unison from cul de sacs up and down the nation, drinking milk from the teat of other animals, and eating creatures that are smarter than our own kids.

But this subjectivity – the way that good and bad, edible and inedible – slip and slide between cultures, is a wonderful thing. It means that, as we drift from place to place, time to time, the things that we take for granted change. What was once unthinkable might become commonplace (look at the growing interest in bug farming, which might bring a future of insect burgers and cricket cookies), and the moral 'certainties' that we carry around with us can disappear in a puff of smoke when we cross borders. This has given us a contradictory, dazzling global patchwork of dog-lovers and dog-eaters, horse-riders and horse-devourers, cow-killers and cow-carers. If you don't come to terms with all this magnificent difference among us, you'll get tied up in knots. Stretch your moral muscles, and wrap your mind around the diversity that shapes our tastebuds. Know that – to someone, somewhere – your food is really fucking weird. Take yourself out of the centre of your moral map, cast off boring ideas of universal right and wrong, and set yourself spinning free: always moving, always changing, obeying your own strange laws of ethics. Plant your feet firm in your principles, but let your body sway in the breeze.

The final bite

A group of people arrived in a new and strange village. Wearied from a long day of travelling, they asked the villagers if they might perhaps give them some food. The suspicious villagers declined and, as evening settled over the little houses, bolted their doors tight. Mobilised by their growling hunger, the travellers hatched a plan. They filled a deep pot with water from the stream, stoked a fire with some sticks and kindling, and began to heat the water. Once the water was shimmering with little rising bubbles, they reverently lowered a large, smooth stone – found half-sunk in the mud of the riverbed – into the pot. The villagers, who had clustered at their windows to see what mischief the outsiders were up to, were baffled.

One villager came out from her house and asked what on earth they were cooking. 'It's stone soup,' said one of the travellers, 'but – I don't suppose you have an onion we could use in it? The soup's a delicacy where we come from, you see, and it needs an onion to work.' The villager wrung her hands and, fuelled by wary curiosity, ran to fetch an onion for the strangers. A little while later, another villager emerged from his house with a grumble and a cough. 'What is this, huh?' 'It's a really special soup – stone soup – from our home town. But do you have a carrot? Just for seasoning, you understand.' The man begrudgingly obliged, before returning to his vantage point at the window, squinting through sceptical eyes.

One by one, more villagers came skulking around the cooking pot, asking questions and bringing, in turn, a sprig of rosemary, a few potatoes, handfuls of greens, a little cut of cured meat and some beans. Before long, the soup was savoury and rich, and the scent of rosemary wafted through the cool dusk air. The travellers looked down at the soup pot and looked to one another with knowing smiles, before gently pulling the stone from the bottom of the pan. They shared the soup in deep bowls long into the night by the dying embers of the fire, the villagers twitching at their curtains in right-eous fury. The next morning the travellers had disappeared, leaving no trace but the cool, round stone sat heavy in the dust.

This folk tale, as weird as it is, has some valuable things to teach us about food, I think. First, trickery will get you everywhere. Second, our curiosity is even greater than our generosity. Third, and most importantly, there is nothing on this earth so useless that it can't, with enough planning and care and resourcefulness, be magicked into something nutri-tious and good. A stone can make soup, if you use it right. Even things that people might label unconscionable – battery eggs, cheap pork sausages, palm oil-based treats – become ambrosial, even life-saving, to a family who can't afford an alternative. Truly, I don't think there's such a thing as crap food if you've got the appetite and the vision to make it work.

All of this is important, because the world is full of people who want to tell you how and when to eat. Most of these people are good, and their advice is ripe with kindness for people, or animals, or the environment – or whatever their moral compass is weighted towards. You might turn to Michael Pollan to learn more about the horror of industrial farming methods. To help you pick apart the doublespeak of the diet industry, Michelle Allison – aka The Fat Nutrition-ist – might be useful, or websites such as Not Plant Based. But each of these voices is interested in one particular facet of morality, and their approach might not always align with what's feasible or desirable for you. There's a lot of fatphobia, for instance, in food writing, and plenty of language that's harmful to those with eating disorders. Even Michael Pollan's famous 'Eat food. Not too much. Mostly plants' ought to be taken with a massive pinch of salt: our economy makes it much more expensive and time-consuming to eat this way than to eat the less virtuous foods that are readily available to us, and I wonder whether the onus would be better put on our government – rather than on us as individuals – to guide, subsidise and provide these kinds of healthy food. Pick carefully at any moralising dogmatism before you internalise it, or it'll rot you from the inside out.

That's why I've avoided telling you what to do here – not because I don't have a set of private moral convictions, or even because I don't think there are things we could all do to be a little better, but because I want you to read those authors who know all about the ins and outs of food, inform yourself, and make decisions that will help those around you. At every mealtime, there are countless people whose mucky little fingerprints weave across our plate. There's our company at the dinner table, of course, who we ought to consider before we choose an expensive restaurant or blithely decide to split the bill. There's also whoever cooked the dinner to consider – if this is you, you probably deserve an extra-large serving and plenty of patience for having sweated for this meal; if the cook isn't you, treat them just the way you'd like to be treated. Think about what kind of discussions you want hanging over your meal, and who you want to nurture. There might be things you could say or do to be extra considerate to people with eating disorders, or things you could learn about to show respect to a host from some other culture. Consider who goes hungry when you set a gold standard, and who's making money from your appetite. When you do these tiny things, the food tastes all the sweeter, not least for you.

And the 'you' here is so incredibly important. This is the 'you' whose tastes have been shaped from those first lazy mouthfuls of amniotic fluid, to funfair sacks of candy floss and Ikea meatballs. You cut your teeth on sweet carrot purée when you were still in nappies, and you built yourself taller, fatter and better with platefuls of fruit and rice and fish. It is you sat there in your skin, reading the words on this page, your mind dense with thought. You, and only you, can pick a path through this treacherous food world. At every step, dilemmas will catch on you like brambles: they will nick your skin, and all of your hunger and humanity will come prickling to the surface in a single spot of blood. And still you sway through, a teetering, tottering jumble of foods patted into an ungainly human shape, doing your best most of the time, and your worst some of the time, and carrying on regardless. Like a baby, you press decisions to your lips and take a bite, and the shape of the situation condenses in your mouth. You are a human animal, feeling your way through all the goodness and badness of the world with a hungry belly. If you can fully inhabit this truth, your belly will rumble with the same cadence as the murmurings of your mind, and your hands will meet knife and fork with perfect coordination, and you will taste the world just as it is. It really does taste good.

Digested: Christmas

'*There are some things in this world that we can set our clocks to,*' *opens Nate, kicking off the Christmas episode of the pop music podcast* Switched On Pop. '*The sun rises and sets, the tides ebb and flow, stars are born and die in fiery novas. And there's one other event in the universe that occurs with inexorable power, and that is that every December, Mariah Carey's* All I Want For Christmas Is You *will be inescapable.*'

Nate isn't wrong. The opening bars of the song shimmy onto the airwaves sometime in late November and proliferate on every major radio station, advert and TV channel, spreading faster than a epidemic of winter flu. The quick 1-2-3-4 beat of those sleigh bells burrows so deep into your brain that by the time the first chorus rolls in, you find your tired winter legs breaking into a canter. Try keeping your cool in a supermarket when it comes on over the radio: what started as a quick milk and bread trip turns into a riotous 'Oooh, Baileys', 'Look at that king prawn party wreath!', 'Shall we get one more Advocaat, just in case?' spending spree, all the while tapping your feet in time with the beat.

More than Bethlehem or Lapland – more than the manger or the church pews or Santa's lap – it's supermarkets where Christmas really happens. They are where so many of the big festive battles are fought: to tinsel or not to tinsel, party platters versus a tray of cocktail sausages, turkey or a more modest chicken and the ever-contentious sprouts. It's in the chaos of the pre-Christmas aisles of Tesco that I've made some of my finest decisions (those Malteser reindeer things) and hit my lowest ebbs (eight extra packs of those Malteser reindeer things). This is the place where so many of us decide what kind of Christmas we're going to have, whether it's a mindful back-to-basics affair or a Tesco Finest blowout.

I'll admit that I struggle to keep my head when the Star-bucks red cups come out and the Coke adverts are on TV. I fully subscribe to the madness: from the first winter rain until the last echo of the tubular bells, a Santa-red mist descends over me, and my rationale goes into hibernation. In those fugue-state supermarket trips and on television and blaring from every speaker up and down the nation, we're encouraged to let loose and enjoy. There's black forest mocha, sticky toffee latte, everything fortified with booze, mince pie ice cream, gingerbread praline, chocolate orange stollen, that Pret Christmas lunch sandwich, Brussels sprouts every way God never intended, peppermint yule log, Quality Street, more booze. It's novel, and it's exciting, and I find myself buying even the most ghastly crap in the spirit of Christmas indulgence.

The way I see Christmas, the whole thing is a national exercise in high camp. Everyone shimmers and sparkles, and it's impossible to find a single item of clothing in any high street store that doesn't have sequins on it for a full two months. All those special edition foods – yule log cream liqueur! – are inversions of the staid, familiar Christmas traditions they draw upon. They take one food genre and mash it into another, so Christmas cake becomes a hot drink, and yule log dessert becomes booze, and a Christmas pudding gets condensed into a chocolate in a selection box. Everything gets distilled to a surreal essence of itself and then repackaged in some new and ridiculous form. It is absurd. It is camp. It is amazing.

But excitement is exhausting. There's a reason why our wide-eyed wonder drains from us as we creak out of youth and *into the drudgery of adulthood: it just uses too much energy to be buzzing all day long. A friend once said we should have Christmas once every four years in the manner of Olympics and World Cups so we don't all keel over from the sheer stress of it. We need moments of mundanity to stay afloat: these boring things smooth over the peaks and troughs to keep us sane. This is what rich tea biscuits and porridge are for. Sometimes it'll be an episode of First Dates that soothes you, or some predictable tweets, or a cuppa. Other times you just need a packet of instant noodles and Brooklyn Nine-Nine reruns. But mundanity doesn't fly at Christmas – it's go big, or go home.*

As Switched On Pop hosts Nate and Charlie go on to discuss in their Christmas special, this constant, enforced state of excitement is practically mandated in Mariah's hit song. In between the brisk tempo and that dusting of sleigh bells and Mariah's soaring vocals, Nate and Charlie point out that there's no verse. The whole song is hook – dancing, spinning, euphoric chorus. Without slower verses to ground it, the song spins anchorless in this hyper-energetic, toe-tapping world of festive excess. Even the song's bridge – a section that might usually provide a contrast to, or a context for, the more dynamic chorus – floats high as Mariah croons that 'everyone is singing, I hear those sleigh bells ringing'. What makes the song both magical and awful is that it condenses the entirety of Christmas – unrelenting cheer and delirium, socially sanctioned indulgence, absolutely no respite from the chaos – into a peppy 3½ minutes. It's no wonder plenty of people are sick of the whole thing barely a week into December.

The whole ordeal is even more fraught if you're someone who struggles with your relationship with food: there's a pressure to constantly eat, ignoring every internal regulatory cue your body gives you. For people who are comfortable with food and eating, this might just mean a harmless Christmas bloat. But if you have a hard time listening to your body's hunger cues, this month of chaotic eating can undermine years of eating-disorder recovery and growth. There's the important matter of money, too, and the fact that merry hedonism is only available to those who can afford the hefty shopping bills it brings. Those with histories of alcoholism may find the omni-booziness of the festive season difficult to weather. The lonely, the bereaved and the sick face a whole raft of anxieties: the compulsory jollity of Christmas leaves a lot of room for disappointment and unmet expectations. When something is this determinedly upbeat, it stands at odds with the grey, up-and-down, meandering realities of our lives.

I'm not advocating that we all ditch the excess and settle for a lump of coal and a clementine this Christmas. I enjoy a kitsch, ridiculous Christmas as much as anyone. I kind of love arriving breathless in January with no idea how I got there or where all the money went. I'm certainly not going to preach at you that you should renounce presents or have a 'tasteful' Christmas without tinsel or snow globes or Celebrations.

But maybe there's something to be said for letting the every-day – the Weetabix and the pasta bakes and the blackcurrant squash – find a foothold in your Christmas time. Make room in your kitchen cupboards for the usual tins of beans, and make sure that you have at least one biscuit in the tin that doesn't have stars or santas on it. Watch a non-Christmas film. Have a coffee that isn't gingerbread flavour.

Do all the normal, useless things that you do all the rest of the year, like not talking to your family, or playing Sims 4, or ordering pizza. Let yourself languish in the peri-Christmas doldrums for a while and be thoroughly bored, if only for a few minutes. Enjoy these moments of nothingness while you can. Let your life be just verse for a while: plodding along, scrolling Instagram with a packet of hobnobs. Because when the chorus comes in and those Mariah sleigh bells starting ringing again, you will find your foot tapping, and your shoulders shimmying, and you'll be dragged into the furore whether you like it or not.

Resources

It's my hope that, somewhere between the covers of this book, you will have read something that resonated with you, and improved the relationship that you have with food. I'm not a doctor or dietitian, psychologist or scientist, though, and I know that there will be plenty of problems that a bit of prose can't solve. In those situations, whether it's poverty or an eating disorder that you're struggling with, it's vital that you seek help from people who really know the score.

The Trussell Trust (www.trusselltrust.org) runs a network of 400 foodbanks up and down the UK. If you're in need of a food package, you can find your nearest branch via their website. Local charities such as **The People's Kitchen** (www.peopleskitchen.co.uk) in Newcastle, or **Bristol Soup Run Trust** (www.bristolsoupruntrust.org.uk), can also help, providing hot meals to those in need. For delicious recipes on a budget, try **Jack Monroe**'s online resources (www.cooking-onabootstrap.com).

For those living with eating disorders, making peace with food can be exceptionally hard. Whether you need help in a crisis or ongoing support towards recovery, eating disorder charity **Beat** (www.beateatingdisorders.org.uk) is there to help. Another specialist eating disorder resource is **Anorexia and Bulimia Care** (www.anorexiabulimiacare.org.uk). **Men Get Eating Disorders Too** (www.mengetedstoo.co.uk) has specialist support for male sufferers. Alternatively, you could check out **Mind** (www.mind.org.uk) for advice relating to anorexia, bulimia or binge eating disorder. Michelle Allison, aka **The Fat Nutritionist** (www.fatnutritionist.com), has loads of really valuable resources on her website, while registered dietitian **Glenys Oyston** (www.daretonotdiet. wordpress.com) could revolutionise your outlook on food, health and weight with her 'health at every size' approach.

There's a lot of complicated and contradictory advice out there about health in this age of wellness, but eating well really doesn't need to be complicated. If you're confused about food and nutrition, the **British Dietetic Association** (www.bda.uk.com) has a few food fact sheets that might simplify things a bit, while the **NHS** (www.nhs.uk) has plenty of information in their Live Well guides. Try not to get too consumed with all the facts and figures, though – remember that your appetite will guide you most of the way, and common sense the rest. If you do have special dietary requirements or find yourself feeling unwell, be sure to consult your GP, or a registered dietitian (nutritionist is a very vague title, and not regulated in the way that 'dietitian' is!), rather than a self-appointed wellness guru.

And finally, if you're stuck for dinner inspiration, or caught in a food rut, here are some of my favourite food writers, to help you fall in love again: **Meera Sodha**, whose cookbook *Fresh India* is my most-cooked-from book ever; **Yemisi Aribisala**, writing about Nigerian food and culture; **Izy Hossack**, whose *The Savvy Cook* tackles health-conscious cooking without the bullshit; **Michael W. Twitty**, who shines a light on the complex intersections of food and race in *The Cooking Gene*; **Laurie Colwin**, whose *Home Cooking* is a perfect portrait of food threaded through real life; and **Nora Ephron**, who makes food fun in her essay collections, *I Remember Nothing* and *I Feel Bad About My Neck*.

Bibliography

Introduction

p. 1 Charles Simic, *The Life of Images: Selected Prose*, reprint edition, New York City, Ecco, 2017.

The magic

p. 8 Tamlin S. Conner, Colin G. DeYoung, Paul J. Silvia, 'Everyday Creative Activity as a Path to Flourishing', *The Journal of Positive Psychology*, online, 2016.

p. 8 Michelle Allison, 'Checking In', *The Fat Nutritionist* [blog], 26 March 2012. Available at: http://www.fatnutritionist.com/index.php/lesson-six-checking-in/.

p. 16 *Waitress*, dir. Adrienne Shelly (Fox Searchlight Pictures), 2007.

p. 18 Sylvia Plath, *The Journals of Sylvia Plath*, New York City, Knopf Doubleday, 2013.

p. 19 Marcella Hazan, *The Essentials of Classic Italian Cooking*, London, Pan Macmillan, 2012.

p. 20 Eric Schulze, 'An Introduction to the Maillard Reaction', *Serious Eats*, 2017 [online]. Available at: http://www.seriouseats.com/2017/04/what-is-maillard-reaction-cooking-science.html.

p. 21 Delia Smith, *Delia's How to Cook*, London, Chivers, 1999.

p. 22 M. F. K. Fisher, *Love in a Dish and Other Pieces*, London, Penguin, 2011.

Hungry human bodies

p. 25 Sir Nathaniel Bacon, *Cookmaid with Still Life of Vegetables and Fruit*, c.1620–25.

p. 25 Leonardo Da Vinci, *The Last Supper*, 1495–8.

p. 27 Michelle Allison, 'How Does Hunger Feel?', *The Fat Nutritionist* [blog], 6 December 2011. Available at: http://www.fatnutritionist.com/index.php/lesson-three-how-does-hunger-feel/.

p. 29 L. Hallberg, E. Björn-Rasmussen, L. Rossander, R. Suwanik, 'Iron Absorption from Southeast Asian Diets', *American Journal of Clinical Nutrition*, vol. 30, 1977, pp. 539–48.

p. 29 E. Björn-Rasmussen, L. Hallberg, B. Magnusson, B. Svanberg, L. Rossander, B. Arvidsson, 'Measurement of Iron Absorption from Composite Meals', *American Journal of Clinical Nutrition*, vol. 29, 1976, pp. 772–8.

p. 29 C. Philpott and D. Boak, 'The Impact of Olfactory Disorders in the United Kingdom', *Chem. Senses*, vol. 39, issue 8, 2014, pp. 711–18.

p. 31 Natasha Campbell-McBride, *Gut and Psychology Syndrome*, Cambridge, Medinform Publishing, 2004.

p. 31 *Ellyn Satter Institute* [online]. Available at: http://www.ellynsatterinstitute.org/.

p. 33 C. B. Pinnock, N. M. Graham, A. Mylvaganam, R. M. Douglas, 'Relationship Between Milk Intake and Mucus Production in Adult Volunteers Challenged with Rhinovirus-2', *American Review of Respiratory Disease*, vol. 141, issue 2, 1990, pp. 352–6.

p. 34 Sheldon Cohen, W. J. Doyle, R. B. Turner, C. M. Alper, D. P. Skoner, 'Emotional Style and Susceptibility to the Common Cold', *Psychosomatic Medicine*, vol. 65, issue 4, 2003, pp. 652–7.

p. 36 M. A. Babizhayev, A. I. Deyev, 'Management of the Virulent Influenza Virus Infection by Oral Formulation of Nonhydrolized Carnosine and Isopeptide of Carnosine

Attenuating Proinflammatory Cytokine-Induced Nitric Oxide Production', *American Journal of Therapeutics*, vol. 19, issue 1, 2012, pp. e25–47.

p. 43 Radhika Sanghani, 'Why This Man Takes Photos of "Women Who Eat On Tubes". He Promises He Isn't a "Weird Deviant"'. *Telegraph*, 7 April 2014 [online]. Available at: http://www.telegraph.co.uk/women/womens-life/10749681/Why-this-man-takes-photos-of-Women-Who-Eat-On-Tubes.-He-promises-he-isnt-a-weird-deviant.html.

p. 44 Lindy West, *Shrill: Notes from a Loud Woman*, London, Hachette, 2016.

p. 45 *Rosemary's Baby*, dir. Roman Polanski (Paramount Pictures), 1968.

p. 45 Anorexia & Bulimia Care, 'Statistics', 2017 [online]. Available at: http://www.anorexiabulimiacare.org.uk/about/statistics.

p. 45 Rachel Moss, 'Two thirds of Brits are on a diet "Most of the Time", Study Shows', *Huffington Post UK*, 10 March 2016 [online]. Available at: http://www.huffingtonpost.co.uk/2016/03/10/majority-brits-are-on-a-diet-most-of-the-time_n_9426086.html.

p. 45 Tobias Otterbring, 'Healthy or Wealthy? Attractive Individuals Induce Sex-Specific Food Preferences', *Food Quality and Preference*, in press, 2017.

p. 47 Heather Havrilesky, 'Ask Polly', *New York Magazine*, 2017 [online]. Available at: http://nymag.com/author/Heather%20Havrilesky/.

p. 47 *Sleepless in Seattle*, dir. Nora Ephron (TriStar Pictures), 2017.

p. 50 Stacy Bias, *Flying While Fat* [animation], 2017. Available at: http://stacybias.net/flying-while-fat-animation/.

p. 50 Taffy Brodesser-Akner, 'Losing it in the Anti-Dieting Age', *The New York Times*, 2 August 2017 [online]. Available at: https://www.nytimes.com/2017/08/02/magazine/

weight-watchers-oprah-losing-it-in-the-anti-dieting-age.
html?_r=0.

p. 51 K. M. Flegal, B. K. Kit, H. Orpana, B. I. Graubard,
'Association of All-Cause Mortality with Overweight and
Obesity Using Standard Body Mass Index Categories: A
Systematic Review and Meta-analysis', *JAMA*, vol. 309, issue
1, 2013, pp. 71–82.

p. 52 Bethany Rutter, Ruby Tandoh, Leah Pritchard (eds.),
'How to Keep Your Brain Together When You're Fat', *Do
What You Want*, Sheffield, Do What You Want, 2017.

You are what you eat?

p. 59 I. Wickelgren, 'Caterpillar Disguise: You Are What You
Eat', *Science News*, vol. 135, issue 5, 1989.

p. 60 Eric Carle, *The Very Hungry Caterpillar*, New York City,
World Publishing Company, 1969.

p. 60 Jean Anthelme Brillat-Savarin, *The Physiology of Taste:
or Meditations on Transcendental Gastronomy*, New York
City, Knopf Doubleday, 2009.

p. 61 Carol Nemeroff and Paul Rozin, '"You are What You
Eat": Applying the Demand-Free "Impressions" Technique
to an Unacknowledged Belief', *Ethos*, vol. 17, issue 1, 1989,
pp. 50–59.

p. 62 Science Museum, 'Doctrine of Signatures', 2017
[online]. Available at: http://www.sciencemuseum.org.uk/
broughttolife/techniques/doctrine.

p. 63 Zoe Adjonyoh, *Zoe's Ghana Kitchen*, London, Mitchell
Beazley, 2017.

p. 64 The New York Times, 'An Official Eating Corps', *The
New York Times*, 31 May 1903.

p. 64 Charlotte England, 'One of UK's Biggest Landlords
Bans "Coloured" People from Renting Properties "because
of the Curry Smell"', *Independent*, 28 March 2017 [online].
Available at: http://www.independent.co.uk/news/uk/

home-news/landlord-bans-coloured-people-curry-smell-
racism-fergus-wilson-kent-a7653851.html.

p. 64 Andrea Freeman, 'Milk, a Symbol of Neo-
Nazi Hate', *The Conversation*, 31 August 2017
[online]. Available at: http://theconversation.com/
milk-a-symbol-of-neo-nazi-hate-83292.

p. 65 Matt Zoller Seitz, 'The Offensive Movie Cliche that
Won't Die', *Salon*, 14 September 2010 [online]. Available at:
http://www.salon.com/2010/09/14/magical_negro_trope/.

p. 65 *Ghost*, dir. Jerry Zucker (Paramount Pictures), 1990.

p. 65 *The Green Mile*, dir. F. Darabont (Castle Rock
Entertainment), 1999.

p. 65 *You Are What You Eat*, pres. Gillian McKeith (Channel
4), 2004–2007.

p. 66 Ben Goldacre, 'What's Wrong with Dr Gillian
McKeith PhD?', *Bad Science*, 18 February 2007 [blog].
Available at: http://www.badscience.net/2007/02/
ms-gillian-mckeith-banned-from-calling-herself-a-doctor/.

p. 67 *Supersize vs Superskinny*, pres. Dr Christian Jessen
(Channel 4), 2008–2014.

p. 67 *Secret Eaters*, pres. Anna Richardson (Channel 4),
2012–2014.

p. 69 *The Holy Qur'an: English Translation, Commentary and
Notes with Full Arabic Text*, 10th edition, Kitab Bhavan,
2001.

p. 69 Marinell James, 'Paging Dr. God: Jewish Views of Illness
and Healing', *Interfaith Family*, 2 September 2009 [blog].
Available at: http://www.interfaithfamily.com/spirituality/
spirituality/Paging_Dr.shtml.

p. 69 Bulkeley, Elizabeth, *A Booke of Hearbes and Receipts*,
Wellcome Library MS 169, 1627.

p. 69 Andreas Vesalius, William F. Richardson, *De Humani
Corporis Fabrica: Book 1 of On the Fabric of the Human
Body: A Translation by William Frank Richardson*,
California, Norman Publishing, 1998.

p. 70 Anthony Warner, 'Want to See Something Really Scary?', *The Angry Chef*, 8 April 2016 [blog]. Available at: http://angry-chef.com/blog/want-to-see-something-really-scary.

p. 71 Ella Mills (Woodward), *Deliciously Ella: Awesome Ingredients, Incredible Food that You and Your Body Will Love*, London, Hachette UK, 2015.

p. 71 Melissa Davey, 'Belle Gibson Misled Public with Cancer Claims, Judge Says'. *Guardian*, 15 March 2017 [online]. Available at: https://www.theguardian.com/australia-news/2017/mar/15/belle-gibson-misled-public-with-cancer-claims-judge-says.

p. 71 Melissa Davey, 'Jessica Ainscough, Australia's "Wellness Warrior", Dies of Cancer Aged 30'. *Guardian*, 1 March 2015 [online]. Available at: https://www.theguardian.com/australia-news/2015/mar/01/jessica-ainscough-australia-wellness-warrior-dies-cancer-aged-30.

p. 72 Beyoncé, *Lemonade* (Parkwood Entertainment/Columbia Records), 2017.

p. 77 Kaitlyn de Graaf and Jennifer M. Kilty, 'You Are What You Eat: Exploring the Relationship Between Women, Food, and Incarceration', *Punishment & Society*, vol. 18, issue 1, 2016, pp. 27–46.

p. 77 Food Behind Bars, 'The Campaign', 2017 [online]. Available at: http://foodbehindbars.co.uk/.

p. 78 HM Inspectorate of Prisons, *Life in Prison: Food*, London, Her Majesty's Inspectorate of Prisons, 2016.

p. 78 Thomas Ugelvik, 'The Hidden Food: Mealtime Resistance and Identity Work in a Norwegian Prison', *Punishment & Society*, vol. 13, issue 1, 2011, 47–63.

p. 78 Roald Dahl, *Matilda*, reprint, London, Penguin, 2016.

p. 78 Margaret Atwood, *The Handmaid's Tale*, revised edition, London, Random House, 2011.

Emotional eating

p. 81 *Blue Is the Warmest Colour*, dir. Abdellatif Kechiche (Wild Bunch), 2013.

p. 82 Judee Sill, *Heart Food* (Water Records), 1973.

p. 83 Helen Fielding, *Bridget Jones's Diary: Picador 40th Anniversary Edition*, London, Pan Macmillan, 2012.

p. 83 *Girls*, written by Lena Dunham (Apatow Productions), 2012–2017.

p. 84 Laurie Colwin, *Home Cooking: A Writer in the Kitchen*, reissue, London, Fig Tree, 2012.

p. 85 *The Great British Bake Off* (BBC), 2010–2016.

p. 90 *The Way We Were*, dir. Sydney Pollack (Columbia Pictures), 1973.

p. 91 Bethany Brookshire, 'Dopamine is…', *Slate*, 2013 [online]. Available at: http://www.slate.com/articles/health_and_science/science/2013/07/what_is_dopamine_love_lust_sex_addiction_gambling_motivation_reward.html.

p. 91 Sarah Lienard, 'What Is the Dopamine Diet?', *BBC Good Food*, 2017 [online]. Available at: https://www.bbcgoodfood.com/howto/guide/what-dopamine-diet.

p. 91 Tom Kerridge, *Tom Kerridge's Dopamine Diet: My Low-carb, Stay-happy Way to Lose Weight*, London, Bloomsbury Publishing, 2017.

p. 92 The British Dietetic Association, *The BDA's Guide to the Latest Diet and Cookery Books in 2017*, 13 January 2017 [online]. Available at: https://www.bda.uk.com/news/view?id=155.

p. 92 The British Dietetic Association, *Food Fact Sheet: Food and Mood*, 2014 [online]. Available at: https://www.bda.uk.com/foodfacts/foodmood.pdf.

p. 93 Goop, 'Jade Eggs for Your Yoni', 2017 [online]. Available at: http://goop.com/better-sex-jade-eggs-for-your-yoni/.

p. 93 Natasha Corrett, 'The Baby Blogs: Month 8',
Honestly Healthy, 2008 [blog]. Available at: http://www.
honestlyhealthyfood.com/baby-blogs-month-8/.

p. 94 *Sex and the City*, created by Darren Star (HBO),
1998–2004.

p. 95 Jordan Sand, 'A Short History of MSG: Good Science,
Bad Science and Taste Cultures', *Gastronomica*, 2005
[online]. Available at: https://faculty.georgetown.edu/sandj/
MSG_Gastronomica_Fall05.pdf.

p. 95 Syllabub, 'Accent on Taste', *Observer*, 22 March 1959.

p. 95 Kwok, 'Chinese-Restaurant Syndrome', *New England
Journal of Medicine*, vol. 278, 1968, p. 796.

p. 95 Alan Levinovitz, *The Gluten Lie: And Other Myths About
What You Eat*, New York, Simon and Schuster, 2015.

p. 96 Stanley Jackson, 'Galen – On Mental Disorders', *Journal
of the History of the Behavioral Sciences*, vol. 5, 1969, pp.
365–84.

p. 100 Michelle Allison, 'Eating Toward Immortality',
The Atlantic, 7 February 2017 [online]. Available at:
https://www.theatlantic.com/health/archive/2017/02/
eating-toward-immortality/515658/.

p. 102 Anorexia & Bulimia Care, 'Statistics', 2017 [online].
Available at: http://www.anorexiabulimiacare.org.uk/about/
statistics.

p. 103 Michelle Allison, 'How to Eat, in a Nutshell – Lesson
One: Permission', *The Fat Nutritionist*, 3 October 2011
[blog]. Available at: http://www.fatnutritionist.com/index.
php/how-to-eat-in-a-nutshell-lesson-one/.

p. 104 'What Is Normal Eating?', *Ellyn Satter Institute*, 2017
[online]. Available at: http://www.ellynsatterinstitute.org/
hte/whatisnormaleating.php.

p. 106 Ray Bradbury, *Dandelion Wine*, New York City,
Doubleday, 1957.

Sharing plates

p. 111 Nora Ephron, *I Remember Nothing*, New York City, Random House, 2010.

p. 112 Janet Maslin, 'I Feel Bad About My Memory', *The New York Times*, 4 November 2010 [online]. Available at: http://www.nytimes.com/2010/11/05/books/05book.html.

p. 113 *When Harry Met Sally*, dir. Rob Reiner (Columbia Pictures), 1989.

p. 113 *Sleepless in Seattle*, dir. Nora Ephron (TriStar Pictures), 1993.

p. 113 *Heartburn*, dir. Mike Nichols (Paramount Pictures), 1986.

p. 114 *Celebrity Big Brother 17* (Channel 5), 2016.

p. 115 *Moonstruck*, dir. Norman Jewison (Metro-Goldwyn-Mayer), 1987.

p. 115 *Charlie and the Chocolate Factory*, dir. Tim Burton (Warner Bros. Pictures), 2005.

p. 115 *The Lunchbox*, dir. Ritesh Batra (Walt Disney Studios Motion Pictures), 2013.

p. 115 *Moonlight*, dir. Barry Jenkins (A24), 2016.

p. 116 John Mbiti, *African Religions and Philosophy*, London, Heinemann, 1990.

p. 117 Bee Wilson, *First Bite: How We Learn to Eat*, London, Fourth Estate, 2015.

p. 123 *Come Dine With Me* (Channel 4), 2005– .

p. 125 Arielle Milkman, 'The Radical Origins of Free Breakfast for Children', *Eater*, 16 February 2016 [online]. Available at: https://www.eater.com/2016/2/16/11002842/free-breakfast-schools-black-panthers.

p. 125 Victoria M. Massie, 'The Most Radical Thing the Black Panthers Did Was Give Kids Free Breakfast', *Vox*, 15 October 2016 [online]. Available at: https://www.vox.com/2016/2/14/10981986/black-panthers-breakfast-beyonce.

p. 126 NewsOne, 'America's Worst 9 Urban Food Deserts', *NewsOne.com*, 22 September 2011

[online]. Available at: https://newsone.com/1540235/
americas-worst-9-urban-food-deserts/.

p. 127 Katie Zavadski, 'Pizza Angels Feed Protesters
at JFK Airport', *The Daily Beast*, 29 January 2017
[online]. Available at: http://www.thedailybeast.com/
pizza-angels-feed-protesters-at-jfk-airport.

p. 127 'What We Do', *The Trussell Trust*, 2017 [online].
Available at: www.trusselltrust.org/what-we-do/.

p. 128 Frank O'Hara, 'Having a Coke with You', in D. Allen
(ed.), *Selected Poems*, 4th revised edition, Manchester,
Carcanet Press Ltd, 2005.

Home cooking

p. 131 M. F. K. Fisher, *The Gastronomical Me*, London, Daunt
Books, 2017.

p. 133 *When Harry Met Sally*, dir. Rob Reiner (Columbia
Pictures), 1989.

p. 133 Nathan Abrams, 'I'll Have Whatever She's Having:
Jewish Food on Film', in Anne L. Bower (ed.), *Reel Food:
Essays on Food and Film*, London, Routledge, 2004.

p. 134 *Annie Hall*, dir. Woody Allen (United Artists), 1977.

p. 134 *Big Night*, dir. Campbell Scott and Stanley Tucci
(Samuel Goldwyn Company), 1996.

p. 135 Zoe Adjonyoh, *Zoe's Ghana Kitchen*, London, Mitchell
Beazley, 2017.

p. 138 *Pulp Fiction*, dir. Quentin Tarantino (Miramax Films),
1994.

p. 138 'Nos Burgers', *McDonald's – France*, 2017 [online].
Available at: https://www.mcdonalds.fr/produits/burgers.

p. 138 'Our Menu', *McDonald's – South Africa*, 2017 [online].
Available at: https://www.mcdonalds.co.za/menu.

p. 138 'Eat – Breakfast', *McDonald's – Pakistan*, 2017 [online].
Available at: https://www.mcdonalds.com.pk/eat#breakfast.

p. 138 'Products', *McDonald's – Russia*, 2017 [online]. Available at: https://mcdonalds.ru/products/106.

p. 139 'Corn Pie', *McDonald's – Thailand*, 2017 [online]. Available at: https://www.mcdonalds.co.th/details. aspx?id=122308.

p. 139 'Products', *McDonald's – India*, 2017 [online]. Available at: https://www.mcdonaldsindia.com/products.html.

p. 139 'Allergeni', *McDonald's – Italy*, 2017 [online]. Available at: http://www.mcdonalds.it/prodotti/allergeni.

p. 139 'What Makes McDonald's', *McDonald's – UK*, 2017 [online]. Available at: http://www.mcdonalds.co.uk/ ukhome/whatmakesmcdonalds/articles/how-are-mcdonalds-beef-burgers-made.html.

p. 139 'About', *McDonald's – Philippines*, 2017 [online]. Available at: https://www.mcdonalds.com.ph/content/page/ about.

p. 140 Samuel Pepys, *The Diaries of Samuel Pepys*, new edition, London, Penguin Classics, 2003.

p. 141 Laura Mason, *Sugar-plums and Sherbet*, London, Prospect Books, 2003.

p. 141 Tim Richardson, *Sweets: A History of Temptation*, London, Bantam, 2003.

p. 142 William Dalrymple, 'The East India Company: The Original Corporate Raiders', *Guardian*, 4 March 2015 [online]. Available at: https:// www.theguardian.com/world/2015/mar/04/ east-india-company-original-corporate-raiders.

p. 142 Stuart Hall, 'Old and New Identities, Old and New Ethnicities', in Anthony D. King (ed.), *Culture, Globalization and the World-System: Contemporary Conditions for the Representation of Identity*, revised edition, Minneapolis, University of Minnesota Press, 1997.

p. 144 Elizabeth David, *A Book of Mediterranean Food*, London, John Lehmann, 1950.

p. 144 Lorraine Chuen, 'Food, Race, and Power: Who Gets to Be an Authority on "Ethnic" Cuisines?' *Intersectional Analyst*, 8 January 2017 [blog]. Available at: http://www.intersectionalanalyst.com/intersectional-analyst/2017/1/7/who-gets-to-be-an-authority-on-ethnic-cuisines.

p. 146 Meera Sodha, *Made in India: Cooked in Britain*, London, Fig Tree, 2014.

p. 146 Soleil Ho, 'Let's Call It Assimilation Food', *Taste*, 26 June 2017 [online]. Available at: https://www.tastecooking.com/lets-call-assimilation-food/.

p. 146 Hayley Silverman, *Cleanliness*, 2015 [sculpture]. Image available at: http://www.hayleysilverman.com/#!/.

p. 147 Dan Lepard, *Short and Sweet*, London, Fourth Estate, 2011.

p. 147 Nigella Lawson, *How to Be a Domestic Goddess: Baking and the Art of Comfort Cooking*, London, Chatto and Windus, 1998.

p. 147 Niki Segnit, *The Flavour Thesaurus*, London, Bloomsbury Publishing, 2010.

p. 149 Kris Jenner, *In the Kitchen with Kris*, New York City, Gallery Books/Karen Hunter Publishing, 2014.

p. 149 Chrissy Teigen, *Cravings*, New York City, Clarkson Potter Publishers, 2016.

p. 150 Mary Berry, *Hamlyn New All Colour Cookbook*, London, Hamlyn, 1987.

p. 152 Lucy Knisley, *Relish: My Life in the Kitchen*, New York City, First Second, 2013.

p. 154 Laurie Colwin, *Home Cooking: A Writer in the Kitchen*, reissue, London, Fig Tree, 2012.

Digested: Food on film

p. 155 *Julie & Julia*, dir. Nora Ephron (Columbia Pictures), 2009.

p. 156 *Chocolat*, dir. Lasse Hallström (Miramax), 2000.

p. 157 *My Big Fat Greek Wedding*, dir. Joel Zwick (Gold Circle
Films), 2002.

p. 157 *Ratatouille*, dir. Brad Bird and Jan Pinkava (Pixar
Animation Studios), 2007.

p. 157 *Mystic Pizza*, dir. Donald Petrie (Night Life Inc. and
Samuel Goldwyn Company), 1988.

p. 158 *Willy Wonka & the Chocolate Factory*, dir. Mel Stuart
(Warner Bros.), 1971.

p. 158 *The Wedding Singer*, dir. Frank Coraci (Juno Pix, New
Line Cinema, Robert Simonds Productions), 1998.

p. 158 *Howl's Moving Castle*, dir. Hayao Miyazaki (Studio
Ghibli), 2004.

p. 158 *Spirited Away*, dir. Hayao Miyazaki (Studio Ghibli),
2001.

p. 158 *Stranger than Fiction*, dir. Marc Forster (Columbia
Pictures), 2006.

p. 158 *It's Complicated*, dir. Nancy Meyers (Universal Pictures),
2009.

p. 158 *The Perfect Man*, dir. Mark Rosman (Universal
Pictures), 2005.

p. 158 *The Lion, The Witch and The Wardrobe*, dir. Andrew
Adamson (Walt Disney Pictures), 2005.

p. 158 *Sweet Bean*, dir. Naomi Kawase (Aeon Entertainment),
2015.

p. 158 *Jiro Dreams of Sushi*, dir. David Gelb (Preferred
Content), 2011.

p. 158 *Babette's Feast*, dir. Gabriel Axel (Panorama Film), 1987.

p. 158 *Chef*, dir. Jon Favreau (Aldamisa Entertainment), 2014.

p. 159 *Tampopo*, dir. Jûzô Itami (Itami Productions), 1985.

Bad taste

p. 162 Nigella Lawson, *How to Be a Domestic Goddess: Baking
and the Art of Comfort Cooking*, London, Chatto and
Windus, 1998.

p. 163 Jon Henley, 'First, Take Your Frozen Mash…',
        Guardian, 14 March 2008 [online]. Available at: https://
        www.theguardian.com/lifeandstyle/2008/mar/14/recipes.
        foodanddrink.

p. 164 Delia Smith, *Delia's How to Cheat at Cooking*, London,
        Ebury Press, 2008.

p. 165 Peter Walker, 'Study Finds 7m Britons in Poverty
        Despite Being from Working Families', *Guardian*, 7
        December 2016 [online]. Available at: https://www.
        theguardian.com/society/2016/dec/07/study-finds-7m-
        britons-in-poverty-despite-being-from-working-families.

p. 165 Jack Monroe, *A Girl Called Jack: 100 Delicious Budget
        Recipes*, London, Michael Joseph, 2014.

p. 165 Caroline Craig and Sophie Missing, *The Cornershop
        Cookbook: Delicious Recipes from Your Local Shop*, London,
        Square Peg, 2015.

p. 169 Joanna Blythman, *SHOPPED: The Shocking Power of
        British Supermarkets*, London, Harper Perennial, 2005.

p. 169 Jon Kelly, 'How First Out-Of-Town Superstore
        Changed the UK', *BBC News Magazine*, 2 September
        2013 [online]. Available at: http://www.bbc.co.uk/news/
        magazine-23900465.

p. 172 J. D. Salinger, *The Catcher in the Rye*, New York City,
        Little, Brown and Company, 1951.

p. 172 Jojo Tulloh, *The Modern Peasant: Adventures in City
        Food*, London, Chatto and Windus, 2013.

p. 173 Marie Kondo, *The Life-Changing Magic of Tidying: A
        Simple, Effective Way to Banish Clutter Forever*, London,
        Vermilion, 2014.

p. 173 Sebastian Faena (photographer), 'Rihanna! The
        Superstar Graces Our March Cover', *Paper* magazine,
        March 2017 [online]. Available at: http://www.papermag.
        com/rihanna-paper-2293524292.html.

p. 174 Kelis, 'Milkshake', *YouTube*, 2009 [video online].
        Available at: https://youtu.be/6AwXKJoKJz4.

p. 174 Beyoncé, *Lemonade* (Parkwood Entertainment/
Columbia Records), 2016.

p. 174 Andy Warhol, *32 Campbell's Soup Cans*, 1962.

p. 174 Katy Perry, 'Bon Appétit (Official) ft. Migos', *YouTube*,
2017 [video online]. Available at: https://youtu.be/
dPI-mRFEIH0.

p. 174 Hannah Marriott, 'Fast-Food Fashion:
Moschino accused of "Glorifying" McDonald's
Logo', *Guardian*, 13 July 2014 [online]. Available at:
https://www.theguardian.com/fashion/2014/jul/13/
moschino-glorifying-mcdonalds-logo-fashion.

p. 174 Suzy Menkes, 'Chanel's Supermarket Chic', *The
New York Times*, 4 March 2014 [online]. Available at:
https://www.nytimes.com/2014/03/05/fashion/chanels-
supermarket-chic.html?_r=0.

p. 175 Chicken Connoisseur, 'The Pengest Munch Ep. 16:
Favourite (Stamford Hill), *YouTube*, 24 March 2017 [video
online]. Available at: https://youtu.be/SOL-fJM2m1I.

p. 176 Chris Perez, 'Tasting Vanilla? It Might Be Beaver Butt.
(And the FDA Approves.)', *The Kitchn*,
19 September 2013 [online]. Available at: http://
www.thekitchn.com/youre-eating-beaver-buttand-the-
fda-approves-195020.

p. 177 Carrie Arnold, 'The Sweet Smell of Chocolate: Sweat,
Cabbage and Beef', *Scientific American*, 31 October 2011
[online]. Available at: https://www.scientificamerican.com/
article/sensomics-chocolate-smell/.

p. 177 David Owen, 'Beyond Taste Buds: The Science of
Delicious', *National Geographic*, December 2015 [online].
Available at: http://www.nationalgeographic.com/
magazine/2015/12/food-science-of-taste/.

p. 178 Bee Wilson, *First Bite: How We Learn to Eat*, London,
Fourth Estate, 2015.

p. 178 Emily Elert, 'FYI: Why Does Some Food Taste Bad to
Some People and Good to Others?', *Popular Science*, 27

March 2012 [online]. Available at: http://www.popsci.com/
science/article/2012-03/fyi-why-does-some-food-taste-bad-
some-people-and-good-others.

p. 179 Understanding Evolution, *Evolution Accounts for Taste*,
September 2014 [online]. Available at: http://evolution.
berkeley.edu/evolibrary/news/140903_hummingbirds.

p. 180 *Eat Well for Less* (BBC Two), 2015– .

p. 181 Alison K. Ventura and John Worobey, 'Early Influences
on the Development of Food Preferences', *Current Biology*,
vol. 23, issue 9, 2013, pp. R401–408.

p. 183 *Strangers on a Train*, dir. Alfred Hitchcock (Warner
Bros.), 1951.

p. 183 David Greven, 'Engorged with Desire: The Films of
Alfred Hitchcock and the Gendered Politics of Eating', in
Anne L. Bower (ed.), *Reel Food: Essays on Food and Film*,
London, Routledge, 2004.

p. 183 Mayukh Sen, 'How – And Why – Did
Fruitcake Become a Slur?', *Food52*, 22 December
2016 [online]. Available at: https://food52.com/
blog/18732-how-and-why-did-fruitcake-become-a-slur.

p. 184 John Birdsall, 'America, Your Food Is So Gay', *Lucky
Peach*, Spring 2014.

p. 184 Charlotte Druckman, 'A Gelato Maestro's
Last Scoop', *Eater*, 30 May 2017 [online]. Available
at: https://www.eater.com/2017/5/30/15691504/
meredith-kurtzman-otto-nyc-gelato.

p. 185 *The Rocky Horror Picture Show*, dir. Jim Sharman
(Twentieth Century Fox), 1975.

p. 186 Roni Caryn Rabin, 'A Hunger Crisis in the
L.G.B.T. Community', *The New York Times*, 18 July
2016 [online]. Available at: https://well.blogs.nytimes.
com/2016/07/18/a-hunger-crisis-in-the-l-g-b-t-community/.

A good egg

p. 187 Tim Richardson, *Sweets: A History of Temptation*, London, Bantam, 2004.

p. 188 Paul Chrystal, *Chocolate: The British Industry*, London, Shire Publications, 2011.

p. 189 Deborah Cadbury, *Chocolate Wars: From Cadbury to Kraft: 200 years of Sweet Success and Bitter Rivalry*, London, HarperPress, 2011.

p. 190 James Robinson, 'Bournville: The Town that Chocolate Built', *Guardian*, 23 January 2010 [online]. Available at: https://www.theguardian.com/business/2010/jan/23/bournville-cadbury-town.

p. 190 Graeme Wearden, 'Timeline: Cadbury's Fight Against Kraft', *Guardian*, 19 January 2010 [online]. Available at: https://www.theguardian.com/business/2010/jan/19/cadbury-kraft-takeover-timeline.

p. 190 Daniel Thomas, 'Is Cadbury's Move the End for Fairtrade?', *BBC News*, 28 November 2016 [online]. Available at: http://www.bbc.co.uk/news/business-38137480.

p. 190 Rebecca Smithers, 'Green & Black's New UK Chocolate Bar Will Be Neither Organic nor Fairtrade', *Guardian*, 3 August 2017 [online]. Available at: https://www.theguardian.com/business/2017/aug/03/green-blacks-new-uk-chocolate-bar-not-organic-fairtrade.

p. 190 Annie Kelly, 'Child labour Is Part of Most of What We Buy Today: What Can We Do?', *Guardian*, 24 November 2016 [online]. Available at: https://www.theguardian.com/sustainable-business/2016/nov/24/child-labour-what-can-we-do-africa-modern-slavery.

p. 190 'Cadbury's Chief Given £4.5 Million Pay Rise', *Telegraph*, 5 April 2013 [online]. Available at: http://www.telegraph.co.uk/finance/newsbysector/retailandconsumer/9973070/Cadburys-chief-given-4.5million-pay-rise.html.

p. 192 *Holy Bible: King James Version*, London, Collins, 2011.

p. 192 Helen Fielding, *Bridget Jones's Diary: Picador 40th Anniversary Edition*, London, Pan Macmillan UK, 2012.

p. 193 'Ancient Theories of Soul', *Stanford Encyclopedia of Philosophy*, 2009 [online]. Available at: https://plato.stanford.edu/entries/ancient-soul/.

p. 193 Gregers Wegener, '"Let Food Be Thy Medicine, and Medicine Be Thy Food": Hippocrates revisited', *Acta Neuropsychiatrica*, vol. 26, issue 1, pp. 1–3.

p. 193 William Gervase Clarence-Smith, *Cocoa and Chocolate, 1765–1914*, London, Routledge, 2003.

p. 193 Charlotte Brontë, *Jane Eyre*, reprint, London, Vintage Classics, 2015.

p. 193 Mark McWilliams, 'Moral Fiber: Bread in Nineteenth-Century America', in Susan Friedland (ed.), *Food and Morality: Proceedings of the Oxford Symposium on Food and Cookery 2007*, London, Prospect Books, 2008.

p. 193 Sylvester Graham, *A Treatise on Bread and Breadmaking*, Boston, Light and Stearns, 1837.

p. 193 Adee Braun, 'Looking to Quell Sexual Urges? Consider the Graham Cracker', *The Atlantic*, 15 January 2014 [online]. Available at: https://www.theatlantic.com/health/archive/2014/01/looking-to-quell-sexual-urges-consider-the-graham-cracker/282769/.

p. 194 *Holy Bible: New International Version*, London, Hodder & Stoughton, 2015.

p. 194 Leon Rappoport, *How We Eat: Appetite, Culture, and the Psychology of Food*, Canada, ECW Press, 2003.

p. 196 Sue Quinn, 'Number of Vegans in Britain Rises by 360% in 10 years', *Telegraph*, 18 May 2016 [online]. Available at: http://www.telegraph.co.uk/food-and-drink/news/number-of-vegans-in-britain-rises-by-360-in-10-years/.

p. 204 Bruce Kraig, 'Why not Eat Pets?', in Susan Friedland (ed.), *Food and Morality: Proceedings of the Oxford Symposium on Food and Cookery 2007*, London, Prospect Books, 2008.

p. 205 Bel S. Castro, 'Food, Morality and Politics: The
Spectacle of Dog-Eating Igorots at the 1904 St. Louis
World Fair', in Susan Friedland (ed.), *Food and Morality:
Proceedings of the Oxford Symposium on Food and Cookery
2007*, London, Prospect Books, 2008.

p. 205 *Meet Me in St. Louis*, dir. Vincente Minelli (Metro-
Goldwyn-Mayer), 1944.

p. 206 Greg Allen, 2004, '"Living Exhibits" at 1904
World's Fair Revisited', *NPR*, 31 May 2004 [online].
Available at: http://www.npr.org/templates/story/story.
php?storyId=1909651.

p. 206 Victor Benno Meyer-Rochow, 'Food Taboos: Their
Origins and Purposes', *Journal of Ethnobiology and
Ethnomedicine*, vol. 5, issue 18, 2009.

p. 209 Stone Soup, *History of the Stone Soup Folktale
from 1720 to Now*, 2017 [online]. Available at:
https://stonesoup.com/about-the-childrens-
art-foundation-and-stone-soup-magazine/
history-of-the-stone-soup-story-from-1720-to-now/.

p. 210 Michael Pollan, *The Omnivore's Dilemma: The
Search for a Perfect Meal in a Fast-Food World*, London,
Bloomsbury Paperbacks, 2011.

p. 210 Michelle Allison, 'Learn to Eat', *The Fat Nutritionist*
[blog]. Available at: http://www.fatnutritionist.com/index.
php/online-nutritionist/.

p. 210 Laura Dennison and Eve Simmons, *Not Plant Based*
[website]. Available at: http://www.notplantbased.com/.

Acknowledgements

Thank you to Cecily Gayford for taking a chance on me and for shaping my vision into this little book. Thanks also to Anna-Marie, Patrick, Flora and Valentina at Profile Books for making this whole project the best that it could possibly be. Many thanks to Stuart Cooper at Metrostar for seeing something of value in this book in the first place, and to Sarah Chatwin for your eagle-eyed edits. Ruby Taylor: I'm so grateful to have had the chance to work with you on this thing that means so much to me. Thank you for bringing it to life with such beautiful art.

There are so many other people who have helped make this book happen – some who contributed directly to the pages in front of you, others who nourished and inspired me with their work, research and writing, and a few who just fed me really great meals. Among them are: Tessa, Åsa, Sheila, my mum, Susan Smillie, Bethany Rutter, Michelle Allison, Meera Sodha, Mayukh Sen, Heather Havrilesky, Soleil Ho and every last person who has ever reached out to me online or IRL and said 'eating feels so fucking complicated sometimes'. Thank you to Leah for loving me and feeding me.

Index

Recipe titles are in *italic*.